OPRAH, MIRACLES,

AND THE

NEW EARTH

BEST-SELLING AUTHOR

ERWIN W. LUTZER

OPRAH, MIRACLES, AND THE NEW EARTH

A CRITIQUE

MOODY PUBLISHERS
CHICAGO

Discussion Questions: Dana Gould
Interior Design: Ragont Design
Cover Design: John Hamilton Design

Library of Congress Cataloging-in-Publication Data

Lutzer, Erwin W.
    Oprah, miracles, and the new earth : a critique / Erwin W. Lutzer.
        p. cm.
    Includes bibliographical references.
    ISBN 978-0-8024-8953-1
    1. Cults. I. Title.
    BP603.L88 2009
    239'.93—dc22

                                                                    2008037486

CONTENTS

WELCOME TO THE
WORLD OF
SPIRITUALITY

THE COSMIC BATTLE

MORE THAN ONE HUNDRED million Americans claim no allegiance to a church, synagogue, or temple. Many of them, perhaps the majority, are pursuing some form of what we'll call Spirituality, hoping to connect with something greater than themselves. They are looking for meaning, seeking for some higher purpose that will fill their inner emptiness and persistent longings for peace. And they are being told that they can do this without believing doctrines, without acknowledging their sins, and without having to commit to believe anything too specific.

Many of these people have been turned off by the church because of what they see as its judgmental attitudes and doctrinaire approach to prescribed teachings and practices. So, as might be expected, they are seeking help elsewhere, based on their own personal needs and inclinations. According to Jerome P. Blaggett, people are saying, "Yes, I want to have a connection to the sacred, but I want to do it on my own terms—terms that honor who I am as a discerning, thoughtful agent and in a way that affirms my day-to-day life."[1]

Martha Sherrill, writing in *O Magazine*, says of this generation of seekers, "We want to feel we're on the road to becoming spiritual beings whose lives are governed by wisdom, compassion and a sense of acceptance."[2] Today people equate Spirituality with growth, experience, and authenticity. They want to be socially aware and Spiritually conscious. It is not an exaggeration to say that a wave of Spiritual energy is sweeping the country. What used to be thought of as a fringe New Age movement is now mainstream.

I'm convinced, however, that there is more to this quest for Spirituality than meets the eye. I believe that while our military experts are concentrating on bombs and missiles, a different kind of battle is being waged for America's heart and soul. Though we think of it as a battle of ideas, it is actually a battle between two supernatural beings who seek the devotion of men. One is referred to in the Bible as "the god of this world," a malicious and cruel being who seeks to enslave his subjects. The other is the living and true God who delights to set people free from the tyranny of sin and meaninglessness.

The eventual outcome of the battle is not in doubt. The god of this world has only as much authority and power as the true God has seen fit to give him. In the end, this wicked spirit will be thrown into the bottomless pit, and be tormented day and night, forever and ever. Satan's days are numbered; his deceptions will come to a bitter end.

Meanwhile, this god whom Christ called "the ruler of this

world" has been granted incredible power to deceive multitudes. And here in America, as the influence of biblical Christianity continues to wane, his power is on the increase. Satan is enlisting people to stand with him in his final assault on God. His message is presented as good news, but beneath the appealing jargon is a massive deception. I write this book to help readers understand how this deception is taking place—under the friendly guise of Spirituality.

THE SATANIC STRATEGY

Let's dream for a while. Suppose you were Satan, burning with a hateful passion to deceive everyone on the face of planet Earth. What if you had the ability to inject thoughts into the minds of some people and tempt others to take your suggestions? What if you were preparing for a final worldwide takeover? Suppose you could do all of your initial planning without being detected. What schemes would you use to get your message across?

Obviously, you would sell your product by providing some tangible dividends without arousing unnecessary fear and attention. You'd package your ideas in a form that the public would accept. All the while, your intentions would have to remain skillfully hidden. Like a fisherman, you'd want to give some immediate gratification but keep the hook out of sight.

Your primary goal is not materialism, immorality, drugs, or despair. There is something else you long for: you want recognition and *worship*. You desire personal contact with humans who will interpret their experience as a meeting with the true God whom you hate. In the end you want them to be willing to take your mark, and pledge loyalty to your schemes. Deception is the name of the game.

To do this, you have to teach that God is impersonal—the

force, energy, and the one all-pervading reality. In fact, *everything* is God. Salvation comes by meditation, by an experience that unites us with the divine. You teach that whereas Christianity says heaven is in the life to come, the good news is that heaven *can't* wait! It is pressing in upon us, simply waiting to be acknowledged and accepted. All around us there are signs that we are entering a new age of peace, where death does not exist and spiritual harmony rules. And we have the potential to make it happen.

And so it is that Satan plies his trade, leading millions to believe that his benefits come, not through the study of doctrine or attending church or even the confession of our sins, but, we are told, through one or more techniques that put us in touch with our "true self." One way or another we can access the basic power of the human mind. By taking a journey within, we can find spiritual reality and fulfillment.

Satan has never lost sight of his long-term goal—the enslavement of multitudes. He wants us to believe that the spirit world around us is a friendly place, and therefore connecting to the supernatural is both beneficial and not to be feared. Satan makes promises like a god—but pays like the Devil.

And one of the most famous promoters of his deceptions is Oprah Winfrey—and several of her guests who teach these doctrines that deceive the masses. It is to her and her friends that we now turn. And we will uncover the lies that are being readily believed by millions.

Prayerfully join me on a journey that might change your life and that of your friends. Step by step we will cover terrain that I pray will help us stay on the right path on our way to the heavenly kingdom.

DISCUSSION QUESTIONS

1. Why is the quest for spirituality such a driving force in our lives? How does the Good News of the gospel uniquely meet our needs in this area?

2. Describe the cosmic battle we find ourselves in. Who are the players, and what forces are involved? What is really behind this battle, and what is at stake?

3. What will be the outcome of this cosmic battle? What does the Bible tell us about the enemy's goals and strategy? (See 1 Peter 5:8–9; 2 Corinthians 11:3, 14–15; Ephesians 6:10–18.)

4. Discuss the points of Satan's strategy in this battle. Relate examples of elements of this strategy you have seen at play in your world of contacts—perhaps even among coworkers and family members.

5. Satan is a master of deception, constantly offering us substitutes for God's truth. What are some of the deceptions and substitutes he offers with New Age Spirituality?

6. One of the philosophies associated with New Age Spirituality is *pantheism*, which teaches that everything is God. In this chapter, Dr. Lutzer briefly touches on a few of its characteristics. Contrast the teachings of the Christian faith of the Bible with pantheism.

Chapter One

MEET OPRAH
AND HER FRIENDS

"THERE ARE MANY PATHS
TO WHAT YOU CALL GOD"
—Oprah Winfrey

"HAVE YOU HEARD about the largest church in the world?"

That was the provocative opening question on a video exposé of Oprah Winfrey's growing obsession with promoting New Age Spirituality. With a daily television audience of millions along with sponsoring *A Course in Miracles* on an XM Satellite Radio program, Oprah has become the high priestess of a new church—some would call it a cult.[1]

The video went on to ask, "What does this new church teach? It requires no belief; heaven is not a location but refers to the inner realm of consciousness. The man on the cross is an archetypical image. He is every man and every woman. What is more, all of us are already holy and we should not make the pathetic error of 'clinging to the old rugged cross.'"

Oprah Winfrey describes herself as a "freethinking" Christian who turned against the traditional teachings of Christianity when she heard her pastor say that "God is a jealous God." She couldn't accept that, she says, because she always thought God was a God of love. This sent her on a quest into Spirituality, to find the true essence of the Christian faith, an essence that is shared by all religions.

Let's hear it in her own words:

And you know, it has been a journey to get to the place where I understand, that what I believe is that Jesus came to show us Christ's consciousness. That Jesus came to show us the way of the heart and that what Jesus was saying that to show us the higher consciousness that we are all talking about here. Jesus came to say, "Look, I'm going to live in the body, in the human body, and I'm going to show you how it's done." These are some principles and some laws that you can use to live by to know that way. And when I started to recognize that, that Jesus didn't come in my belief, even as a Christian, I don't believe that Jesus came to start Christianity . . . well, I'm a Christian who believes that there are certainly many more paths to God other than Christianity.[2]

Oprah is one of America's most respected and most admired spiritual gurus. I realize, of course, that to be critical of what Oprah says or does, is, in the minds of many, to be critical of the divine. Indeed, *USA Today* ran an article titled "The Divine Miss Winfrey?"[3] To her credit, she lavishly gives money for many philanthropic causes, and through her "Angel Network" and the "Use Your Life Award" she has made a difference in the lives of many children. She had funded scholarships for black colleges, written checks to churches, and moved families out of the inner city.

More recently she has used her wealth to build a school for disadvantaged children in Africa.

Because Oprah was sexually abused as a child she is able to empathize with those who suffer and particularly those who have experienced the same fate. She has courageously taken on issues such as domestic violence and marital infidelity; she has pulled back the curtain and helped liberate the secrecy and expose the reality of these important themes.

So far, so good.

Why should we be interested in what Oprah believes about Jesus and the divine? After all, she does not claim to be a pastor or preacher. She does not have a degree in theology and makes no claim to being a biblical scholar. To her credit, she does not hold herself up as a god; she is just doing what she does, or more accurately, what she feels called to do. She is at the top or near the top of any list of the most admired women in the world. She connects with millions every day and we dare not ignore her influence.

OPRAH'S INFLUENCE

Oprah has millions who follow her teachings on Spirituality. The article in *USA Today* says, "After two decades of searching for her authentic self—exploring New Age theories, giving away cars, trotting out fat, recommending good books and tackling countless issues from serious to frivolous—Oprah Winfrey has risen to a new level of guru."

To continue, "Over the past year Winfrey has emerged as a spiritual leader for the new millennium, a moral voice of authority for the nation." She has used her pulpit, says Kathryn Lofton, and so "Oprah has emerged as a symbolic figurehead of spirituality."[4]

If we doubt her impact on her twenty to fifty million viewers each week, we should be reminded that a poll on Beliefnet. com reports that 33 percent of the respondents say that she had a more profound spiritual impact on them than their clergy persons. Cathleen Falsani, religion writer for the *Chicago Sun-Times* asks, "I wonder, has Oprah become America's pastor?

"I think that if this were the equivalent of the Middle Ages and we were to fast-forward 1,200 years, scholars would definitely think that this Oprah person was a deity, if not a canonized being."[5] Marcia Nelson, who has written a book on Oprah, says that she is today's Billy Graham.[6]

Because of the long list of New Age teachers she promotes on her media outlets, she has done more to promote New Age Spirituality than any other person on planet Earth. And she appears to believe what she promotes. When she recommends a book on her book club, sales soar. And recently she has taken to promoting three of the present leading gurus of New Age religion.

Let's meet a few of her more recent friends.

ECKHART TOLLE

Eckhart Tolle is the author of two influential books, *The Power of Now: A Guide to Spiritual Enlightenment* and *A New Earth: Awakening to Your Life's Purpose.* Although these books cover essentially the same themes, each gives a slightly different slant to his understanding of Spirituality. Oprah has given most of her attention to *A New Earth* on her TV show, but she has also joined with Tolle on a live Web-based event accessed by hundreds of thousands of people, anxious to learn how they can be awakened. Along with the information there are testimonies of people whose lives have been changed as a result of applying these principles.

Tolle was born in Germany and at the age of thirteen moved

to Spain with his father. He became interested in literature and astronomy. He says, "Even as a child I could already feel what later would become periods of intense depression—even as a child I would sometimes think, How can I eliminate myself from this world? How can I commit suicide? And was working out possibilities to do it."[7] At the age of fifteen he read books written by a German mystic that opened him up to another dimension of consciousness. Later he graduated from the University of London and became a research scholar at Cambridge University.

At the age of twenty-nine he had a profound "conversion," a spiritual transformation that dissolved his old identity and radically changed the course of his life. When he could no longer live with himself, he realized that he was conscious of his thoughts —there were actually two of him, not just one. He was able to separate this "consciousness" from his ego (the outer thought forms) and he found peace. He realized that there was a parallel universe into which he could retreat that not only made his problems bearable but actually gave him a quiet sense of presence or "beingness."

The next few years were spent integrating what he had learned with his own life and then sharing the results with others. He came to realize, he says, that the New Testament had a deeper meaning, and he knew intuitively that some statements attributed to Jesus were added later. After these discoveries he became known as a spiritual teacher and a healer. He was largely unknown until Oprah began to promote him and his books, which she said had changed her life.

A New Earth has sold millions of copies; indeed, the speed of sales has surpassed all other books. "What we're seeing now is so beyond what a bestseller is, it is really a phenomenon," says the publisher. Oprah says, "Being able to share this material with you is a gift and a part of the fulfillment of my life's purpose . . . it was an awakening for me that I want for you too."[8]

What do we make of his insights and conversion? Later in this book we will discuss these teachings in more detail. For now, I will simply say that their origin actually dates back to an early chapter in the book of Genesis. The underlying assumptions and teachings are as old as occult religion. What Tolle discovered is a spirit world characterized by deception and demonic attachment.

RHONDA BYRNE

Australian-born Rhonda Byrne wrote a book titled *The Secret*, which was heavily promoted by Oprah. Byrne's life had collapsed around her, and through searching for answers she discovered that she uncovered the greatest "secret" in history. When she began practicing this secret, her life began to change in ways that were nothing short of miraculous. She was convinced that a variety of famous people discovered "the secret," which transformed their lives. She decided to make a video called *The Secret* to share her discoveries with others. A DVD then led to the publication of a book, which with Oprah's help was catapulted to the top of the charts back in February 2007.

The essence of this secret is "the law of attraction." According to Byrne, the Universe (always capitalized because it is synonymous with God) vibrates on a particular frequency. When you think of something in harmony with the frequency, you attract it to you. If you think wealth, you will receive wealth; if you think about debt, you will be further in debt. "Nothing can come into your experience unless you summon it through persistent thoughts."[9]

Byrne promises with ironclad certainty, "There isn't a single thing that you cannot do with this knowledge. . . . The Secret can give you whatever you want."[10] The claims that are made for

The Secret are so grandiose that we will be tempted to smile. The whole universe is at our disposal; it is waiting for us to attract untold blessings. All this and more is ours if only we are open to it!

In promoting *The Secret* Oprah says, "It has been marketed and packaged in such a way that people of our generation, of this time, can receive it in a way that perhaps they couldn't have received it from other philosophers."[11] Millions believe that the key to financial advancement, health, and opportunity are found within the pages of this mega-bestseller. Whether this is so will become clear in the chapters that follow.

HELEN SCHUCMAN

Although Helen Schucman is now deceased, she is the author of the book *A Course in Miracles*, which is taught on satellite radio by Marianne Williamson through Oprah's inspiration and encouragement. We can't understand Williamson and her worldwide impact unless we know how Schucman's book came about.

In October of 1965, Schucman, a Jewish atheist psychologist and associate professor of medical psychology at Columbia University in New York, began receiving channeled messages from an unknown spirit guide that claimed to be the voice of Jesus. She and a colleague began by writing down the dreams Schucman had, and this prepared her for what followed.

Within time Schucman became accustomed to "the voice," which gave her a rapid inner dictation that she took down in shorthand. And although she could stop the process at any time, she continued to act as a scribe, writing what was dictated to her. In her words, "It made me very uncomfortable, but it never seriously occurred to me to stop. It seemed to be a special assignment I had somehow, somewhere agreed to complete." The result was a long, convoluted book titled *A Course in Miracles*.

We should note in passing that this kind of automatic writing, which bypasses the consciousness of the writer, is common in occult circles. The writer's hand forms the words, but the person is unaware of what will be written. Sometimes this writing is done in a trance; at other times the writer is aware of his/her surroundings, but the author passively receives the message from an unseen entity. One of the best-known automatic writers was Helene Smith, an early twentieth-century psychic who felt that her automatic writing was an attempt by Martians to communicate with Earth. She claimed she could translate the Martian language into French.

As in other occult writings, *A Course in Miracles* stresses that what you believe is unimportant, and even irrelevant. What is important is the technique, the application of ideas that will put you in touch with a higher form of consciousness. The book says that we can never agree on what to believe, but fortunately, that is unimportant; what is important is the inner core of our own being that unifies all religions and religious experiences.

We should point out that this is not only a form of brainwashing, but also is consistent with Hinduism, which stresses technique, not specific beliefs. Listen to what the spirit guide dictated to Helen Schucman to write:

Some of the ideas the workbook presents you will find hard to believe, and others may seem to be quite startling. This does not matter. You are merely asked to apply the ideas as you are directed to do. You are not asked to judge them at all. You are asked only to use them. It is their use that will give them meaning to you, and will show you that they are true.

Remember only this; you need not believe the ideas, you need not accept them, and you need not even welcome them. Some of them you may actively resist. None of this will matter, or decrease their efficacy. But do not allow yourself to make exceptions in applying the ideas the workbook contains, and whatever your reaction to the ideas may be, use them. Nothing more than that is required.[12]

Imagine, we are told that the book will not interfere with anyone's religion! Its ideas and techniques can harmonize with whatever we believe. I will explain the basic themes and ideas found in *A Course in Miracles* in the succeeding pages. Having spent many hours perusing the book, I can say with confidence that when you pick it up, you are, in effect, holding a version of *The Satanic Bible*. It attacks everything taught in Scripture, especially the atonement and the work of Jesus on the cross. There are powerful reasons to believe that "the entity" that dictated the book was an evil spirit—a demon—who knew much more about Christianity than Schucman could have known; and whatever the demon knew, he hated with a vengeance.

MARIANNE WILLIAMSON

Marianne Williamson has written a popular exposition of *A Course on Miracles* entitled *A Return to Love*. Since Williamson herself was profoundly changed by the course, she began teaching seminars on it and today is a recognized expert in propounding its teachings. The original book written by Helen Schucman contains 365 lessons, one for every day, and this formed the basis for teaching the course on XM radio to millions of people. Those who took the course will have learned many things such as the following:

Lesson #35, "My mind is part of God's. I am very holy."
Lesson #38, "There is nothing my holiness cannot do."

Lesson #61, "I am the light of the world."
Lesson #96, "Salvation comes from my one Self."
Lesson #186, "Salvation of the world depends on me."
Lesson #191, "I am the holy Son of God Himself."

What about Williamson herself? She is well acquainted with the realm of demonic spirits and sees herself as a witch. In her words:

> During the wee hours of the morning, both angels and demons take shape. . . . In those hours that I've lain so inconveniently awake, I think I've begun at last to know what awakened means. Noting the witching hour—4:15—at which I awake more often than not, stealing outside to look at the stars and marvel at the moon, I return again to my ancient self. In those hours, I am not a menopausal nutcase, I'm a magical witch, and I can feel it in my bones.[13]

Exactly what Williamson says about the huge issues of life—God, heaven, death, and the like—will become clear later. For now, we must simply grasp the fact that *A Course in Miracles* is an exercise in occultism, the dark side of the spirit world.

Eckhart Tolle, Rhonda Byrne, and Marianne Williamson are at present the three most prominent friends that Oprah has recommended to her vast audience. Of course, she has promoted many New Agers in the past, such as Gary Zukav and the writings of Eric Butterworth; but these three have, thanks to Oprah, extended their influence around the world.

THE PURPOSE OF THIS BOOK

By the time you are reading this book, Oprah might be promoting some other author or book that claims to unlock the key to spiritual experience. So in these pages, I want to introduce you to basic principles of discernment that will be of benefit regardless of who the next guru of Spirituality will be. Occultism, no matter its form, always has certain telltale teachings by which it can be identified. In fact, as we shall see, these lies can be traced all the way back to the garden of Eden. It is not just that these ideas are incompatible with Christianity; these are powerful teachings that have their origin in rebellion against God. This is not, as one person thought, "Christianity Lite"; it is a satanic counterfeit.

I write this book for those Christians who thought that the antidote to their own spiritual dryness is to plumb the depths of these teachings. I write for the Christian woman I met who bought Tolle's book *The New Earth* to share with a friend because she thought that it would help both of them in their own spiritual journey! I write for those who have forgotten that Satan sometimes transforms himself into an angel of light.

Don't be fooled because of the use of words such as *Jesus, love, peace, reconciliation,* and *atonement.* These biblical words and others like them are given radically different definitions; it's equivalent to calling good evil and evil good. Visualize a bottle clearly labeled: Drinking Water. Then imagine someone emptying the bottle and filling it with a clear liquid poison. The label still remains, but the contents are disastrous to anyone who dares take even a sip. In these occult writings, the words are there, but the meanings are entirely different.

Truth for all of its power does have this limitation: there is only one way to be right but many ways to be wrong! There is only one right answer to the equation two plus two equals four. But there are almost an infinite number of wrong answers to the equation! Just so, there are many ways to be wrong about matters of spirituality, but at root, all of these errors can be reduced to four or five lies. And error can be more easily recognized when you know what you are looking for. I pray that this book will be a primer on discernment. Like a friend of mine says, we have to *learn* to *discern*.

Also, my prayer is that this book will fall into the hands of many who have already been beguiled by the New Spirituality. I write for the confused person who has tried these techniques, but is unsure about whether he/she has as yet attained enlightenment or experienced an awakening. I also write for the person who has plunged deeply into this unseen realm, only to experience moments of exhilaration as well as moments of despair.

C. S. Lewis was right: "We all want progress. But progress means getting nearer to the place where you want to be. And if you have taken a wrong turning, then to go forward does not get you any nearer. If you are on the wrong road, progress means doing an about-turn and walking back to the right road; and in that case the man who turns back soonest is the most progressive man."[14]

I write, praying that we shall be guided by God's Word.

"Now the Spirit expressly says that in later times some will depart from the faith by devoting themselves to deceitful spirits and teachings of demons" (1 Timothy 4:1).

"Do not despise prophecies, but test everything; hold fast what is good. Abstain from every form of evil" (1 Thessalonians 5:20–22).

Let's begin a journey that begins in Eden but ends with the triumphant return of Jesus Christ, King of kings, Lord of lords. Let's ponder the characteristics of deception and walk toward the One who is the "light of life" (John 8:12).

DISCUSSION QUESTIONS

1. Have you been drawn to or influenced by Oprah Winfrey's promotion of New Age Spirituality? If so, what about it attracted you?

2. Why does Dr. Lutzer view Oprah Winfrey's vast influence as a grave concern? To what extent has she been able to spread the teachings of those she promotes?

3. In this chapter, Dr. Lutzer interacts with four authors and their books, *A New Earth, The Secret, A Course in Miracles,* and *A Return to Love.* Have you read any of those books? If so, which book or books? What were your impressions?

4. Briefly discuss the basic idea of Eckhart Tolle's book *A New Earth.* What is really behind his awakening? To what has he succumbed?

5. What is the point of Rhonda Byrne's book *The Secret?* What about it attracts people to its message?

6. What are the origin and premise of Helen Schucman's *A Course in Miracles?* Why does Dr. Lutzer compare it with *The Satanic Bible?*

7. Briefly describe Marianne Williamson's *A Return to Love.* What is dangerous about the content of her teachings?

8. In this chapter, Dr. Lutzer presents the purpose for his book. What are some of the cautions he gives his readers regarding the New Age Spirituality movement?

9. What benefits might we gain and what truths might we learn from Dr. Lutzer's book? (See 1 Timothy 4:1; 1 Thessalonians 5:20–22; John 8:12.)

Chapter 2

REDEFINING
GOD

"I MYSELF AM THE RULER OF THE UNIVERSE"
—*A Course in Miracles*

IF IT IS TRUE that no religion can rise higher than its conception of God, we must be clear as to what we believe about the divine being. So when the serpent said to Adam and Eve "you will be like God," what did this creature have in mind, and more important, how would Adam and Eve have interpreted this reassuring reply? Understanding this satanic promise opens up the whole world of Spirituality.

Obviously, Adam and Eve could not have the attributes of sovereignty and omnipresence; they could not have created the trees in the garden of Eden nor the starry heavens above. God would have to be redefined if Adam and Eve were to resemble Him. God would have to be pared down to correspond to Adam and Eve's limitations and experience. God could not be thought of as existing apart from them, but as residing *in* them. Even more to their liking, they would participate in godhood.

And so, in one act of disobedience, Adam and Eve moved into the center of their world to usurp God's role. But as Paul Tripp points out, "The 'you can be like God' offer in the garden was not an honest invitation to more; it was a deceitful trick that would only lead to less."[1] Here, in the first recorded episode of satanic deception, we find the origin of the radically different conception of God found in the New Spirituality. That, in brief, explains how the satanic promise made in Genesis is fulfilled in books such as *A Course in Miracles*, which tells us to proclaim, "My mind is part of God's. I am very holy."[2]

This redefinition of God lies at the heart of all occult religion from Hinduism to Mormonism and from the Masons to Eckhart Tolle. God is remade to our liking and specifications. In fact, the God who exists agrees with us on every point. He not only is very much like us; we are so much like Him that we are, in essence, God Himself.

THREE VIEWS OF GOD

There are basically three different views of God, and each religious belief is but a variation of these three conceptions. Today, all three understandings of God vie for the allegiance of men.

Theism is the belief that God is the creator and sustainer of the universe. The Judeo-Christian tradition best exemplifies this understanding of who God is; He is personal, powerful, and independent of the universe. He is creator, and a God to whom we must give an account. And because He is both personal and just, He will eventually bring every individual into judgment so that righteousness will eventually prevail.

Atheism is the view that there is no God. The final reality is believed to be matter, not spirit. In fact, there is no spiritual aspect to the world. There are no souls; there are no spirits that survive independently of the body, no angels, demons, or mystical realities. Atheism denies the possibility of life after death and insists that miracles cannot occur. Perhaps atheism is best expressed in the now-famous line of the late Carl Sagan in his book *Cosmos*: "The cosmos is all there ever was and is, and all there ever will be."[3]

But there is a third conception of God called *pantheism*, a belief extensively developed in Eastern mysticism and also enthusiastically endorsed by Oprah's friends. As I've mentioned, Adam and Eve could not have believed that they would be "like God" in the sense that He is the creator of the world, the sun, and all that exists within the universe. But if they affirmed that nature was God—if they believed that God is all that exists—then they also could think of themselves as God. Thus in succeeding centuries, pantheism was refined and expanded and finds its most detailed expression in Hinduism.

Pantheism is most easily defined as the belief that "God is all, and all is God." The word *pan* means *all* and, as such, refers to the idea that all that exists is God; there are merely different levels of existence that correspond to different levels of divinity. The lowest level is matter; then comes the vegetable kingdom, followed by the animal kingdom, and finally mankind. But everything is God. Nature is God; you are God; I am God. God is all that there is.

It is this pantheistic conception of God that forms the basis for the New Spirituality. Statements that we would attribute to God and Jesus are attributed to us as human beings, because, after all, we are deity. When Marianne Williamson and Oprah were teaching *A Course in Miracles*, they would have come to lesson #191, which boldly declares, "I am the holy Son of God Himself."[4] We are assured that when we say these words all illusions will end, and light will come into the crevices of our souls.

Here are a few other lessons that say essentially the same thing: Lesson #70 teaches, "My salvation comes from me."[5] Lesson #186 teaches, "Salvation of the world depends on me."[6] In lesson #61, we are asked to repeat the affirmation, "I am the light of the world."[7] Thus to affirm God is to affirm ourselves.

Similarly, Eckhart Tolle writes, "God . . . is formless consciousness and the essence of who you are."[8] Tolle takes statements about God and Jesus and applies them to us. According to him, the Jesus of the New Testament is not unique; He might have understood His divinity better than we do, but, says Tolle, whatever is said in the Gospels about Jesus can be said about us.

Read Tolle's words for yourself:

> The Truth is inseparable from who you are. Yes, you *are* the Truth. If you look for it elsewhere, you will be deceived every time. The very being that you are is truth. Jesus tried to convey that "I am the way and the truth and the life." These words uttered by Jesus are one of the most powerful and direct pointers to the Truth if understood correctly. If misinterpreted, however, they become a great obstacle. *Jesus speaks of the innermost I Am, the essence identity of every man and woman, every life-form, in fact. He speaks of the life that you are.*[9] (italics added)

So, please notice that you and I are also "the way, the truth, and the life." Quite conveniently, Tolle omits the rest of what Jesus said. The entire verse reads, "I am the way, and the truth, and the life. *No one comes to the Father except through me*" (John 14:6, italics added). Tolle says that if we interpreted these words in a way that affirms the uniqueness of Jesus, we have "a great obstacle." Of course, many of us as Christians affirm that it is exactly this "great obstacle" that leads to the heart of the gospel. But I'm ahead of the story.

After Tolle's "conversion," he says he immediately understood the New Testament at a deeper level and knew intuitively that "certain statements attributed to Jesus were added later because they did not emanate from a state of consciousness."[10] In another context Tolle says, "What is the mind of God? Consciousness . . . through the present moment you have access to life itself, which has been traditionally called God."[11] The bottom line is that God is simply our own consciousness.

So the God of Oprah's friends is found not by searching outside of ourselves, but going deeply into our own minds, into our own consciousness. There we discover a God whom we need not fear, an impersonal God to whom we do not have to give an account. Marianne Williamson put it this way: "For many people, God is a frightening concept. Asking God for help doesn't seem very comforting if we think of Him as something outside ourselves, or capricious or judgmental. But God is love. We were created in His image, or mine, which means we are extensions of His love. This is why we are called the sons of God."[12]

When Williamson says that we were "created in His image," we should not interpret this to mean that there was a point when God created all things in a biblical sense. Rather, we must understand that we are co-creators with God. Therefore, the word *creation* means simply that since God is all there is, it follows that to say that God is creator is to simply affirm the existence of everything there is. And since we exist, we are a part of the consciousness called God.

Listen to Williamson explain it: "The concept of the divine or 'Christ' mind, is the idea that, at our core, we are not just identical, but actually the same being. 'There is only one begotten son' doesn't mean that someone else was it, and we're not. It means we're all it. There is only one of us here."[13] She allows no distinction between us and Christ. When we focus on Christ, she says, we should simply focus "on the goodness and power that is latent within us, in order to invoke them into realization and expression."[14]

Armed with these insights, we can now boast of being like God. We can take our seat on the throne of the universe. We can quote lesson #38 in *A Course in Miracles* and tell ourselves, "There is nothing my holiness cannot do."[15]

The consequences of taking God's place are, of course, conveniently hidden from those who are bent on believing in their own divinity. With this deception, the serpent's promise, "you will be like God," appears to be fulfilled. Delusions are substituted for reality and the truth is set aside with a lie. And the consequences go on for all eternity.

FALLING INTO THE POOL

Narcissus, it is said, was so enamored with the reflection of his face as he gazed into a pool that in a moment of self-absorption, he fell into the water! Just so, we have today an inordinate fascination with one's self: self-admiration and even self-worship. Probably there is no narcissistic teaching that can rival that of Australian author Rhonda Byrne, who wrote the mega-bestseller *The Secret*, a book, as we've noted, heavily promoted by Oprah Winfrey.

The secret to everything, she insists, is "the law of attraction." She, along with her co-contributors, teaches that everything in the Universe (which is always capitalized and usually synonymous for God) vibrates on a particular frequency. When you think in harmony with the frequency of something, you attract it to you.

"Nothing can come into your experience unless you summon it through persistent thoughts."[16]

This elevation of ourselves sets the stage for the final deification of humanity. Speaking about us as humans, she writes, "You are God in a physical body. You are a spirit in the flesh. You are eternal life expressing itself as you. You are a cosmic being. You are all powerful. You are all wisdom. You are all intelligence. You are perfection. You are magnificence. You are the creator, and You are creating the creation of You on this planet."[17] Christianity has always taught that Jesus was God in the flesh; according to Byrne, we are all God in the flesh—God in a physical body.

Now comes the most grandiose exercise of self-worship imaginable. She says that if we as humans only understood "the secret" we would know that:

The earth turns on its orbit for You. The oceans ebb and flow for You. The birds sing for You. The sun rises and it sets for You. The stars come out for You. Every beautiful thing You see, every wondrous thing You experience, is all there for You. Take a look around. None of it can exist, without You. No matter who you thought you were, now you know the truth of who you really are. You are the master of the universe. You are the heir to the kingdom. You are the perfection of life. And now you know the secret.[18]

Think of it: words that should be addressed to the God of heaven are addressed to us—yes, they are addressed to the person you see every day when you look into the mirror. Such teachings only fuel the imagination of this generation that is drowning in an ocean of narcissistic self-worship! I'm reminded of the T-shirt with the words, "Just worship me and we'll get along just fine."

Let me say again that one sure mark of all occult religion is that man is deified, usurping the place of God. There is no doubt that the demonic spirit who dictated *A Course in Miracles* is of the same ilk as the spirit who gave Joseph Smith and other prophets of Mormonism special revelations. Thus, we should not be surprised that Mormonism teaches, "As man is, God once was: as God is, man may become."[19] Many similar quotations can be cited that emphasize that we can attain godhood. Satanic religion always invites us to make a claim to our own deity. "You will be like God," the serpent promised. And today, millions still believe him.

The Deity of Mankind is the lie Satan has always been anxious to pass on to gullible human beings who are eager to believe it!

SIN DOES NOT EXIST

Ideas have consequences. Once you affirm that we are already holy—that we are already God, then it is quite impossible to accept our sinfulness. Unlike Christianity that teaches that we are separated from God because of our sin, the New Spirituality teaches that we are, in fact, already united with God. So, although you and I think that we are separated from God because we are conscious of sin and regrets, we are now told that we were never separated from God at all. The deeper we go within ourselves, the more we are invited to deny our guilt and pain and find peace within.

So, predictably, there is no mention of sin in *The Secret*. No need to mention sin since the Universe, and all of us, are already "perfect." The cause of all the problems in the world is merely bad thinking, especially the failure to recognize and appropriately use "the law of attraction." Therefore the solution to what we call our problems lies within us. The only "savior" we need is ourselves.

Along the same vein, Eckhart Tolle denies that sin exists, but admits that we are afflicted with a dysfunction—a dysfunction of the ego, which ultimately does not really exist. What many of us consider to be evil, according to Tolle, is really only an illusion, a bad dream. "The deeper interconnectedness of all things and events implies that the mental labels of 'good' and 'bad' are ultimately illusionary. They always imply a limited perspective and so are true only relatively and temporarily."[20]

Lesson #337 in *A Course in Miracles* says, "My sinlessness protects me from all harm." Then it goes on to explain, "My sinlessness ensures me perfect peace, eternal safety, everlasting love, freedom forever from all thought of loss; complete deliverance from suffering. And only happiness can be my state for only happiness is given me."[21] The lesson ends with a prayer affirming that "I was mistaken when I thought I sinned, but I accept atonement for myself." So, if you think you are a sinner, you are just mistaken. No sin means no coming judgment.

If you have followed the argument so far, we have learned that we are God, so we are entirely holy and therefore sin does not exist. It follows that human beings are not responsible for what they do, even if what they do is sometimes called (erroneously) evil. In a later chapter, I will quote Tolle, who makes the point that we cannot hold human beings responsible for their behavior. What we call evil happens in the body; and since only the realm of the spirit is real, we cannot hold others accountable for their actions, which are really illusory. Our real self cannot be separated from God because the real self is a part of God. "You do not become good by trying to be good, but by finding the goodness that is already in you, and allowing the goodness to emerge. But it can only emerge if something fundamental changes in your state of consciousness."[22]

According to Tolle, truth cannot be found in thought, doctrines, or narratives, which are perceived through our egos. "Every ego confuses opinions and viewpoints with facts. It cannot tell the difference between an event and its reaction to that event. Only through awareness—not through thinking—can you differentiate between fact and opinion . . . only thorough awareness can you see the totality of the situation or person instead of adopting one limited perspective."[23]

I can't help pointing out that if truth cannot be found in "thought, doctrines, or narratives," how can it be found in Tolle's own book *The New Earth*? Although truth is not something you believe, Tolle apparently makes an exception for his own writings! He has written hundreds of pages to convince us to believe certain thoughts, doctrines, and narratives. Clearly, he expects us to set reason aside when it comes to understanding his point of view; we must embrace irrationality to experience the "awakening."

No wonder Calvin says that the mind is an idol factory, constantly shaping images of God that are either unworthy of Him or radically wrong. There is an old adage that says that God created man in His own image—and now man has returned the favor.

THE CONTRAST

The concept of God in New Spirituality is about as far from the God of the Bible as one can travel. The desire of man to form God into an image he can live with is indisputable proof of man's rebellion and unrepentant pride. Obviously, the enterprise is a farce: imagine the silliness of man affirming that the kind of deity he wants is the kind that actually exists! Think of the hubris of identifying God with one's basic desires and aspirations (consciousness) and then saying that this God is the *real* God. Add to that the audacity of saying that we all participate in this divine essence.

Wouldn't it be better to investigate to see if there is evidence that there is a God beyond the world who is its creator and judge? The biblical conception of God fits the facts of both history and science. And for that matter, the Christian worldview gives us the most rational understanding of the world and our place in it.

The apostle Paul was certainly inspired by God when he made this prediction: "For the time is coming when people will not endure sound teaching, but having itching ears they will accumulate for themselves teachers to suit their own passions, and will turn away from listening to the truth and wander off into myths" (2 Timothy 4:3–4). Yes, today people do not want to listen to the truth but wander off into myths.

The God of the Bible is not found by getting in touch with our own consciousness, but rather by looking at His revelation in the person of Jesus Christ. This God is one who is seen in nature and, more important, by reading the Scriptures. There we see God's transcendence, His power to create, and to sustain what He has created. The imaginary God of the New Spirituality can be debunked in so much as a single quotation from the Bible:

> To whom then will you compare me, that I should be like him? says the Holy One. Lift up your eyes on high and see: who created these? He who brings out their host by number, calling them all by name, by the greatness of his might, and because he is strong in power not one is missing. (Isaiah 40:25–26)

Take a moment to ponder these two verses and see how they contradict modern Spirituality. In this simple paragraph of Scripture, we learn that (1) it is folly for us to think we are like God; we dare not compare ourselves with Him. When we think of God, we should not look for similarities, but rather contrasts between us and the Almighty. Then we learn that (2) He created the worlds at a point in time; we are *not* co-creators with Him, for we ourselves are His creation; and (3) He is personal, calling even the stars by name. This means that He also knows us in terrifying detail, even keeping track of the number of hair on our heads (Matthew 10:30). Finally, He is (4) sovereign over His entire creation; which means He is sovereign over us too.

The New Spirituality is nothing less than idolatry of the heart, which is just as serious as idolatry of the hand. Already in Ezekiel's time, the prophet warned, "Son of man, these men have taken their idols into their hearts, and set the stumbling block of their iniquity before their faces" (Ezekiel 14:3). The passage goes on to speak about the coming judgment of those who would redefine God, making Him into an idol they can control. The God of the New Spirituality is an idol created in the human heart in a frantic search for peace of mind. At it turns out, this God just happens to be the figment of an eager but thoughtless imagination.

"These things you have done, and I have been silent; *you thought that I was one like yourself.* But now I rebuke you and lay the charge before you" (Psalm 50:21, italics added).

ENOUGH SAID.

DISCUSSION QUESTIONS

1. How is God redefined by occult movements such as the New Age Spirituality? Discuss the three views of God we see today. What is the basic premise of each?

2. What was "the lie" that Satan gave Adam and Eve in the garden of Eden? How do we see this deception played out today in our everyday world?

3. Drawing from what we see in Eckhart Tolle's and Marianne Williamson's writings, in what ways does pantheism form the basis for New Age Spirituality? What does pantheism teach?

4. Discuss this quote from Dr. Lutzer: "Delusions are substituted for reality and the truth is set aside with a lie. And the consequences go on for all eternity." We confront Satan's delusions daily. When confronting Satan's delusions, what are some steps we can take to reject them and embrace God's truth?

5. What is author Rhonda Byrne's "secret" to everything? Drawing from the brief discussion in this chapter, describe the essence of her secret—"the law of attraction."

6. Common to the writings of the authors under discussion, "sin" is a concept that is redefined and explained away. What are the implications of such a teaching?

7. Dr. Lutzer alludes to John Calvin's idea that "the mind is an idol factory, constantly shaping images of God that are either unworthy of Him or radically wrong." How imperative is it for us to be governed by the Bible's teachings about the nature of God, rather than our own images of Him? What traps might we fall into if we do not adhere to biblical teaching about God's nature?

8. Contrast the concept of God in New Spirituality with the God of the Bible. What do 2 Timothy 4:3–4 and Isaiah 40:25–26 tell us?

Chapter 3

REDEFINING
CONVERSION

"THERE IS NO NEED FOR HELP TO ENTER
HEAVEN, FOR YOU HAVE NEVER LEFT"
—A Course in Miracles

HEAVEN, ACCORDING TO *A Course in Miracles*, like everything else, exists only within our own minds. If we don't feel as if we are in heaven at this moment, we can remedy that by a "transformation of consciousness." Tolle writes, "We need to understand here that heaven is not a location but refers to the inner realm of consciousness."[1] He says to enter this realm we need a shift in consciousness; we need to separate our egos from our inner consciousness.

To use an analogy, let us suppose that our present reality is represented as being on channel 5 on our television, but if we switch to channel 7 we discover a different reality. In this new order of consciousness, we discover that there is a "parallel universe" where we find peace and the ability to accept whatever comes our way. We learn to live in the *now*, unburdened by the future and refusing to accept the reality of our perceived pain.

We must remind ourselves, however, that the Devil has always wanted to duplicate God's work. Whatever God does, He does as best He can. Jesus taught the need to be "born again" to enter the kingdom of heaven. The New Spirituality teaches that we must be converted, born into a new realm of existence. To accomplish this, we need to enter into our inner consciousness and thus enter into another dimension, beyond the world of sense perception. Once we have this experience, we move from darkness into light, and our intuition now guides us.

This enlightenment was promised back in Genesis chapter 3. When Satan came to Adam and Eve, he persuaded them to make their own decisions without consulting God. To do this, the man and the woman had to learn to trust their own intuitions rather than obey a clear command. In return, their "eyes [would] be opened," and they would experience enlightenment. The scheme worked. "When the woman saw that the tree was good for food, and that it was a delight to the eyes, and that the tree was to be desired to make one wise, she took of its fruit and ate, and she also gave to her husband who was with her, and he ate" (Genesis 3:6).

With her own eyes opened, she would no longer have to depend on God's guidance. And, after a manner of speaking, the serpent's promise came to pass. Adam's and Eve's eyes were opened and they experienced a new order of reality: the downside was that they now had the horrid experience of sin with all of its corruption and pain. The promised enlightenment was darkness of the first order. From then on, Satan's ultimate desire for us is not to commit immorality or even to look to astrology for guidance or to be healed by crystals. All these techniques of the New Age Movement are but stepping-stones to his most subtle deception, namely, the duplication of religious experience.

Eckhart Tolle tells us that our inner purpose is to "awaken," to experience this shift in consciousness. In fact, the subtitle to his book *The New Earth* is *Awakening to Your Life's Purpose*. He himself felt so hopeless and despondent that he was about to commit suicide. But on one memorable evening he discovered that there was another dimension, a realm of the mind beyond consciousness that he could enter with his thoughts. There in the *now* he was given peace and hope. He submitted himself to a higher power.

When he had his awakening, he says it was like being sucked into a hole. But a voice within said, "Resist nothing." So he let go. "It was almost like I was being sucked into a void, not an external void, but a void within. And then fear disappeared and there was nothing that I remember after that except waking up in the morning in a state of total and complete 'newness.'" Later he knew intuitively that certain statements attributed to Jesus in the New Testament were added later.[2]

A Course in Miracles says that its teachings are a course in mind training and it is dedicated to "thought reversal"—to showing us how to change our perceptions so that we can see things differently. Through disregarding the ideas that are in the mind and drifting into another dimension of consciousness, we can enter into a new sphere—namely, the realm of spirit—and thus be free from our bodies and egos that are constantly standing in the way of our personal peace and happiness.

When Satan fell he said he would be "like the Most High" (Isaiah 14:14). His ultimate desire is for humans to encounter him and think they are in touch with the living God. The bottom line is that he wants to give his followers a "satanic conversion." He thinks this miracle is proof that he is succeeding! To effect a spiritual conversion is his most dazzling deception!

Think of the audacity of Satan's attempt to get us to duplicate what Christ has said! Jesus Christ said, "I am the light of the world" (John 8:12; 9:5). Lesson #61 in *A Course in Miracles* instructs *us* to make that same claim: "I am the light of the world." Again, Christ promised special knowledge to those who believe on Him: "This is eternal life, that they may know You, the only true God, and Jesus Christ whom You have sent" (John 17:3 NASB). True to form, Satan promises that his followers can have secret knowledge that makes them members of an elite group. Lesson #33 says, "There is another way of looking at the world," and it explains how we can change our perceptions. Eckhart Tolle says that if you find his book incomprehensible or meaningless, "it has not yet happened to you."[3]

Here again Spirituality turns out to be a revival of the "mystery religions" popular during the pagan days of Greece and Rome. It was based on the idea that there was secret knowledge that could be obtained by searching the depths of one's own soul. Through mystical encounters with cosmic powers, enlightenment was possible.

SALVATION WITHOUT JESUS

Does Jesus have anything to do with our healing or salvation? *A Course in Miracles* gives the answer: "The name of Jesus Christ as such is but a symbol. It is a symbol that is safely used as a replacement for the many names of all the gods to which you pray."[4]

The blood of Christ is belittled and is deemed unnecessary for salvation. *A Course in Miracles* includes a section titled "Atonement Without Sacrifice," claiming that the notion of sacrifice is totally unknown to God: "Those who represent the lamb as blood stained do not understand the meaning of the symbol; it is a very simple symbol that speaks of my innocence."[5] It then explains that to believe that there was a sacrifice for sins is a notion born of fear.

What about the cross of Christ? Listen to these words of stinging rebuke given to us as Christians, "The journey to the cross should be the last useless journey. Do not dwell upon it, but dismiss it as accomplished. . . . Do not make the pathetic error of clinging to the old rugged cross. Until then you are free to crucify yourself as often as you choose. . . . We have another journey to undertake, and if you will read these lessons carefully they will help prepare you to undertake it."[6]

We must pause for a breath. How would Helen Schucman, who grew up as an atheistic Jew—how would she know about the song "The Old Rugged Cross"? This hymn, written in the year 1913 by George Bennard, is seldom sung today. Truth be told, Schucman probably didn't know the hymn, but she didn't have to know it in order to ridicule it! Remember, she was just a scribe for the spirit guide, that inner voice who dictated *A Course in Miracles*.

For the benefit of those who don't know this treasured hymn, here is the first stanza and the chorus that contains the words quoted above:

On a hill, far away, stood an old rugged cross
The emblem of suffering and shame
And I love that old cross
Where the dearest and best
For a world of lost sinners was slain

So I'll cherish the old rugged cross
Till my trophies at last I lay down
I will cling to the old rugged cross
And exchange it some day for a crown.

Thus the demon who dictated the book to Schucman daringly mocked the cross of Christ, saying that those who "cling to the old rugged cross" are making a "pathetic error." Be assured Satan hates the cross, because there he was defeated. Speaking of Jesus, the Scripture says that on the cross, "He disarmed the rulers and authorities and put them to open shame, by triumphing over them in him" (Colossians 2:15). Paul affirmed, "But far be it from me to boast except in the cross of our Lord Jesus Christ, by which the world has been crucified to me, and I to the world" (Galatians 6:14).

The New Spirituality sees everything differently. Williamson speaks about "accepting Christ," but gives it a new twist. According to her it means, "I accept the beauty within me as who I really am. I am not my weakness. I am not my anger. I am not my small mindedness. I am so much more and I am willing to be reminded of who I really am."[7] We do not come to Christ as sinners; we go within ourselves, and there we find whatever perfections we need to connect to our higher consciousness. In other words, we bring about our own transformation.

A SATANIC CONVERSION

The promoters of New Spirituality assume that any connection to the spiritual realm is positive; all supernatural forces are good and in our best interest. They do not realize that there is a spiritual realm that is not committed to God's side in the cosmic struggle. Our universe is in a state of civil war; God's rule is being challenged, and today we live in enemy territory. In fact, the whole world lies in the lap of evil. And, as we shall see, any kind of self-salvation leads us into darkness that masquerades as light.

The Bible teaches that the earth is populated with spirit beings called demons, who are only too happy to communicate information and become a seeker's guide. Many people falsely believe that demons communicate only evil ideas, not realizing that these spirits may often give good advice and even mouth sound doctrine. When our Lord was on earth, demons frequently confessed that He was the Christ. Interestingly, when a demon-possessed slave girl followed Paul around the city of Philippi, she kept saying, "These men are bond-servants of the Most High God, who are proclaiming to you the way of salvation" (Acts 16:17 NASB). Her "spirit of divination," as the Bible calls it, was meticulously correct in its assessment. Yet a few days later, Paul cast the spirit from the girl.

Demons are liars who receive perverted satisfaction from deceiving gullible humans. When the truth serves their purposes, they will use it; when half-truths are called for, they have them in their arsenal; but lying is their most popular weapon. Quite possibly they are assigned to certain individuals and, because they study the behavior and history of their subject, they become very knowledgeable regarding his or her past. After the person has died, these spirits are open to the possibility of communicating with relatives and friends who want to have a conversation with their departed loved one. A channeler is contacted who purports to "call up" the dead and establish communication. But, in fact, the communication is not with the dead, but with demons who impersonate the dead.

It is this realm that we enter when we seek to have our internal awakening, which comes about by opening the mind to the spirit world. This transformation is nothing less than an encounter with another spiritual being. In his book *The Seat of the Soul* Gary Zukav (a frequent guest on Oprah's show) tells us, "You will draw to yourself, as you have, guides that can provide you with just this assistance. They appear to be such that we can give them names, or speak to them as though they were other personalities."[8]

C. S. Lewis perceptively realized that the highest form of deception would be for demons to duplicate spiritual experiences.

The fictional demon Screwtape, in giving instructions to his underling Wormwood, says, "I have great hopes that we shall learn in due time how to emotionalize and mythologize their science to such an extent that what is, in effect, a belief in us, (though not under that name) will creep in while the human mind remains closed to belief in the Enemy [God]."[9]

Think of the sinister delight Satan has when taking the place of God in the life of an individual, even to the point of granting his client a spiritual conversion! This explains why those who have had this initiation are so convinced they alone have the right perception of reality. They think they are plugged into the energy of the Universe and have been reconciled to a pantheistic god who is indeed all there is. How can they be so sure? They've *experienced* it! They believe in the infallibility of their feelings.

Satan is the leader of these multiplied millions of demons. That's why counterfeit conversions can take place anywhere, anytime. How does one enter into this esoteric encounter, the experience of enlightenment? There are many paths that lead to the demonic kingdom.

HOW DOES IT HAPPEN?

According to Tolle, this transformation begins with "detachment," which in turn leads to "inner space." When encountering any difficulty, we should simply say, "This too will pass." To quote him, "This, too, will pass, brings detachment and with detachment another dimension comes into your life—inner space."[10] You must suspend all judgment, either of right or wrong, or your own assessment of who you are. Then you will see the impermanence of the things around you, and you will be ready to enter into a new reality. There in this "space" you will actually transcend thought. Passivity—a commitment to judge nothing—is key in finding your inner space.

Let me quote Tolle in more detail:

> Awakening is a shift in consciousness in which thinking and awareness separate. . . . Even those rare beings who experience a sudden, dramatic and seemingly irreversible awakening will still go through a process in which the new state of consciousness gradually flows into and transforms everything they do and so becomes integrated into their lives.[11]

In *A Course in Miracles*, this conversion comes by chanting and repeating various affirmations. For example, you should repeat these words, "I am the holy Son of God Himself" (Lesson #191). When you repeat this, the promise is that you are "released from the bondage of this world." And in this one truth all illusions are gone, and at last you are free, and everything has changed. Just speak the words and "A miracle has lighted up all dark and ancient caverns, where the rites of death echoed since time began." And the promise doesn't end there. With these words you can then say, "All power is given unto you in earth and Heaven. There is nothing that you cannot do." Thus, you will be transformed into the new dimension.[12]

On the Web, Marianne Williamson will actually tell you what you should say on any given day and how many times it should be repeated. She follows the instructions in *A Course in Miracles*, where technique and rote procedure are enjoined as the method of transformation. Hinduism teaches much the same method, stressing that one must empty the mind by means of meditation. Then the will is immobilized and the mind will make contact with the inner consciousness.

Rationality is actually a hindrance to this mystical unity with God; indeed, if we have various beliefs we are actually insane, or mad.[13] As long as I am thinking about something, I perceive my-self to be distinct from the objects of this world. So I must have an experience in which such distinctions disappear, so that I might lose my identity like a drop of water in the vast ocean of impersonal energy. To achieve this, I empty the mind.

Thus Tolle agrees with Hinduism that what a person believes is not important. Indeed, it would be best if we just had no beliefs —because all such specific ideas shut us off from ultimate reality. We remember the admonition in *A Course in Miracles*: You don't have to believe anything, but just follow the prescribed proce-dure. And after you have embarked on your new journey, your re-ligious beliefs fall away like leaves from a dead tree. So you can believe whatever you like, but eventually if you follow the lead of the guru, you will soon get beyond doctrinal beliefs.

Surrendering the will breaks down our resistance to making contact with a foreign power. When we concentrate on a poem or solving a problem, we focus on various associations of images and thoughts. Since such thinking is a barrier to unity with the one all-inclusive reality, the ultimate goal of meditation is the de-struction of human rationality. The mind no longer thinks of anything, but is absorbed with the One Reality.

At this point, the mind has miraculous powers over natural objects and receives special revelations. As you continue, you will proceed toward that stage where your inner self will shine forth in its own light and self-illumination. For some, this conversion experience comes more easily than it does for others.

When we attain a state of "pure consciousness," we go *be-yond* personality, *beyond* morality, and *beyond* knowledge. Satan's conversion experience is complete—the transformation of con-sciousness has occurred. There is only abstract unity, a state that approaches total oblivion. Enlightenment, we are told, has at last been achieved.

CONTRAST JESUS AND THE NEW BIRTH

When Jesus said, "Unless one is born again he cannot see the kingdom of God" (John 3:3), He was speaking about an entirely different conversion. For one thing, this conversion is done for us by God; it most assuredly is not something that we achieve. We are to be "born from above" by a miracle performed by a personal God. What is more, this conversion does not ask us to empty our minds, but rather to believe certain doctrines about ourselves, about Christ, and about God. Specifically, we must see ourselves as sinners who need the reconciliation that Christ alone can bring.

Two humans can beget a child in their own likeness, morally and physically (we've all marveled at how strikingly similar a child can look like his father or mother). Just so, God begets us in His own likeness. Don't get me wrong. God always remains God, and we always remain human; but when we are born again, we do receive His nature. We don't become perfect in our everyday living, but we are made different.

Neither you nor I can give the new birth to anyone! We are begotten by God alone without human assistance. There are many things we can do, but bringing about the new birth is not one of them. When God regenerates, He is acting though the Word and the Spirit. The new birth is a direct act of omnipotence!

This should clinch it for us. Paul wrote, "Therefore if anyone is in Christ, he is a new creature; the old things passed away; behold, new things have come" (2 Corinthians 5:17 NASB). Scientists have done many wonderful things, but one thing they have never done is create so much as a single molecule. Creation is God's work and we can only stand in awe of His power. He creates ex nihilo, that is, out of nothing. Even if we had been living on the day when the heavens and the earth were created, He would not have needed us to make His job easier. No need for our help because it was just a bit much for the Almighty. No, He acted alone, and with good reason.

When we are "born again," we are given a new nature that had no existence before God created it within us. Light, of course, was also created by divine fiat. Just so, the spiritual light that produces the new birth is the sovereign work of God. "For God, who said, 'Light shall shine out of darkness,' is the One who has shone in our hearts to give the Light of the knowledge of the glory of God in the face of Christ" (2 Corinthians 4:6 NASB). The shaft of light that causes us to be reborn has to come from God.

IS JESUS NECESSARY?

I conclude with this question: Is Jesus—the Jesus of the New Testament—necessary for the new birth and our reconciliation with God? On an Oprah Winfrey show one member of the discussion—evidently arguing for Christianity—said that there are two forces in the world: God and the power of darkness.[14]

Oprah asked whether we can choose between the two. The panel member responded, "Absolutely."

Oprah then commented that one of the mistakes we make is to believe that there is only one way to live—"but there are diverse beings in the world."

The panel member asked, "How do you please God?"

Oprah answered, "There are many ways and many paths to what you call God. And her path might be something else when she gets there and she might call it the light but her loving and her kindness and her generosity brings her. . . . If it brings her to the same point that it brings you, it doesn't matter if she calls it God along the way or not."

The panel member responded that there is only one way to

God, but Oprah argued differently—there could not possibly be one way.

The discussion progressed, and then Oprah asked this provocative question: *"Does God care about your heart, or does God care about if you call His Son Jesus?"*

This is a critical question. What she is asking is, "Is it possible to have your heart right before God even if you don't accept Jesus as the only path to God?" And given the context of the question and Oprah's other comments about Jesus, it is quite clear that she intended a positive answer. In other words, if we are good people—if our heart is right—it doesn't matter whether we call God's Son Jesus. Any other path would do. As long as your heart is right, the content of your faith does not matter very much.

But—and here is where Oprah and her friends miss it—there cannot be many ways to the divine, for the New Spirituality fails in its hapless attempt to define sin out of existence. But the more seriously we take sin, the more desperately we need a Savior.

The reason that many think we can be reconciled to whatever God or gods there be is because the modern mind does not encourage moral reproach; it especially does not encourage self-reproach. Pride is no longer viewed with alarm but is praised and cultivated. Just think back over the comments made about our divinity in the writings of the New Spirituality!

Honesty forces us to confess that we are unable to assess the true state of our souls. We are obsessed with self-protection and self-aggrandizement. But if we are willing to listen to our conscience, we must admit that sin is a deadly burden to the soul. Left to ourselves, we are really lost.

But God—the God of the Bible—is impeccably just. He cannot allow bygones to be bygones. Sin is a personal affront to a personal God. His nature demands that sin must be paid for, either by the sinner or someone who stands in his/her stead. Our own sin is so serious that if we have to pay for it ourselves, we will be suffering eternally in hell. But Jesus, the second Person of the Trinity, came to die in our place and suffered our eternal penalty in His six hours on the cross. Now He not only takes away our sin but gives us His righteousness—the very righteousness we need for God to receive us. And when we receive that gift, we are "born again."

If you've followed this so far, you know that God demands perfect holiness from us, and in Jesus *God supplies what He demands!*

Let's return to Oprah's question: Is God more interested in our heart than if we call His Son Jesus? The answer is this: God is interested in our hearts—indeed, that is the focus of His attention, *but we cannot have a clean heart unless we call His Son Jesus.*

Self-salvation doesn't work for sinners. If you try to wash a dirty well with water from the same well, it will never get clean. To think that we, by our own efforts, are able to cleanse our hearts is folly indeed. And denying our sin—as we are encouraged to do —is hardly honest.

As a woman told me on the telephone, "I cannot take steel wool to my heart to scrub it!" No, she can't, and neither can we. She needs a forgiving God to enter deep within her psyche and cleanse her within. Thankfully, she accepted God's Son to do it.

The New Testament tells us about a Jesus you can trust; indeed, He is a Jesus you must trust if you expect to be forgiven and "born again." So, if you have never received Christ as Savior and Redeemer, this would be a good time to do so. "But to all who did receive him, who believed in his name, he gave the right to become children of God" (John 1:12).

WE ARE REAL SINNERS. WE NEED A REAL SAVIOR.

DISCUSSION QUESTIONS

1. How does the concept of heaven revealed in *A Course in Miracles* and Eckhart Tolle's writings differ from the biblical view of heaven?
2. Why does *A Course in Miracles* emphasize "thought reversal"? What does this thought reversal involve?
3. Helen Schucman's writings reject Christ's sacrifice on the cross as unnecessary. Contrast that with what we read of the power of the cross in 1 Corinthians 1:18 and Colossians 2:13–15.
4. What do we know about the spirit beings we call demons? How do they work to undermine God's truth?
5. How does a counterfeit spiritual conversion happen? Read 2 Corinthians 5:17 and 2 Corinthians 4:6–7. Contrast the spiritual conversion experience described by Tolle and *A Course in Miracles* with the new birth in Christ.
6. Discuss the question posed on an Oprah TV show: "Does God care about your heart, or does God care about if you call His Son Jesus?" and Dr. Lutzer's ensuing discussion in this chapter. Is the Jesus of the New Testament necessary for the new birth and our reconciliation with God? (Read John 1:12.)

Chapter 4

REDEFINING
DEATH

"DEATH IS THE CENTRAL DREAM
FROM WHICH ALL ILLUSIONS STEM"
—*A Course in Miracles*

JUST IMAGINE FOR A MOMENT that you see yourself as a part of the collective consciousness that we call "God." Since you are in charge of your own destiny, and make your own reality, there is no obstacle that you cannot overcome. Peace of mind, fulfillment, and happiness are yours by virtue of who you are. You've bought into the lie, so now you have to make it work.

But standing in the path of this cheery journey toward self-realization is the nasty obstacle called *death*. The knowledge of our mortality, as it is generally understood, is a serious blow to our "godhood." Strictly speaking, as God, we should be able to rid ourselves of the humiliation that seems to come with our own demise. Only if we master death can we continue to proclaim our own divinity.

God told Adam and Eve that if they would eat of the fruit of the forbidden tree, they would "surely die" (Genesis 2:17). Of course, this couple could not have grasped what death really meant, since there was no example of death in the perfect world they had experienced. But it should have been clear to them that death was a punishment of some kind; no matter how good the fruit tasted, the negative consequences would soon outweigh any possible benefit that the fruit could bring.

Enter the serpent.

The serpent directly defied God's word. He assured Adam and Eve, "You will *not* surely die" (Genesis 3:4, italics added) and he said this with enough confidence to get Eve to believe him. The two "revelations" Eve received could not be more at odds. God said, "You will die," and the serpent said, "You will not die." Flat-out contradiction!

Who was right? In the aftermath of the disobedience, it appeared as if the serpent was right—Adam and Eve ate the forbidden fruit and they did not die. The next morning the sky was still blue; they could watch the animals scurry about as they walked amid the beautiful trees of the garden. The one immediate difference is that they now felt shame; they even went into hiding to cover their nakedness.

Clearly, they didn't die physically, at least not immediately. Their bodies were still functioning, but the process of death had begun its perilous journey. As George Bernard Shaw is frequently quoted as saying, the statistics on death are impressive; it is one out of one. From now on, all of their offspring would be born with an expiration date.

Although physical death didn't take place on that day, spiritual death did. On the very day that they ate the forbidden fruit, they found themselves cut off from God, alienated from His presence. Rather than looking forward to their walk with the

Almighty in the garden, He now had to call to them and ask them why they were hiding. When confronted, Adam was not forthright about his disobedience, but blamed it on the woman, who in turn blamed it on the serpent. And, as some wag said, "The serpent didn't have a leg to stand on."

Like it or not, death was now a reality. This was proof that man cannot take God's place in the world, no matter how hard he tries. True, he is created in God's image and as such has personality and creativity. But he can never exchange places with God, and all disobedience to God's commands have dire consequences. Man's very existence was dependent on God.

But the serpent that promised Adam and Eve that they would not die continues to make the same promise today, even in the face of overwhelming evidence to the contrary. *A Course in Miracles* teaches that death is an illusion. It says, "But if there is reality in life, death is denied. No compromise in this is possible."[1] It goes on to say that if we were to die, God would die, for remember, our collective consciousness is God.

Since the denial of death is a critical component of occult teachings, let's consider it in more detail. As we shall see, this lie has far-reaching implications.

THE DENIAL OF DEATH

A Course in Miracles speaks of death in several places, but keeps repeating that it is an illusion, a dream for which we need not prepare, for our only future is in the now. "Atonement might be equated with total escape from the past and total lack of interest in the future. Heaven is here. There is nowhere else. Heaven is now."[2] So, contrary to what is generally believed, death is only a delusion that ultimately leads us nowhere. Heaven is here.

When *A Course in Miracles* says that death is the dream from which all other illusions stem, it is assuming the notion that the physical realm is not real; only the spiritual exists. Denying death is necessary, we learn, if we are to affirm life. To quote again, "Death denies life. But if there is reality in life, death is denied. No compromise in this is possible."[3] Indeed, if death is real, then it is impossible for us to think of God as loving. But because God is not a God of fear but of love, death cannot exist. Lesson #163 reads, "There is no death. The Son of God is free."[4]

Teachers of *A Course in Miracles* are solemnly told, "Teacher of God, your one assignment could be stated thus; accept no compromise in which death plays a part. Do not believe in cruelty, nor let attack conceal the truth from you. What seems to die has but been misperceived and carried to illusion. Now it becomes your task to let the illusion be carried to the truth."[5]

How is this denial of death to be sustained? We are told that someday we will agree that nothing occurs outside our minds. "How a person seems to show up for us is intimately connected to how we choose to show up for them."[6] So, it turns out that death exists only in our own minds; since the mind is the true reality, then physical death with all of its attendant humiliation simply does not exist. Yes, there might be funeral homes and cemeteries, but they are only an illusion, a dream from which we must awake.

Eckhart Tolle says he never thinks of death because if you live in the "now" you need not worry about the future! He agrees that heaven is here; it is the inner realm of consciousness. "This is the esoteric meaning of the word, and this is also the meaning in the teachings of Jesus."[7] A new heaven is the emergence of a transformed state of human consciousness.

If death is denied, quite obviously sickness does not exist. *A Course in Miracles* says, "If God created you perfect, you *are* perfect. If you believe you can be sick, you have placed other gods before Him."[8] If we have an unclouded mind, we will know that sickness does not exist.

So what should we do when we are sick?

TALKING TO YOUR AIDS VIRUS

Marianne Williamson, in an attempt to interpret *A Course in Miracles*, bravely tries to show that the mind has power over disease and that we do not have to accept what we think is happening to us. She says that AIDS patients can speak to their viruses to reassure themselves that this disease is really under their control. After all, we are the sum of our thoughts, and if we just think rightly, the disease will be brought under the spell of our own power.

Please read this "conversation" between Steve and his AIDS virus. In context, Steve has written a letter to the virus expressing his fear. In turn, the virus wants to reassure Steve that it/she/he was not out to "get Steve" but rather to teach Steve that he has power over this virus.

The virus is speaking:

> If I was, as they say, out to get you, don't you think you would be dead by now? I am not able to kill, harm, or make you sick. I have no brain, brute strength or great harming force. I am just a virus. You give me the power you should give to God. I take what I can because I don't want to die any more than you do. Yes, I live off your fears. But I die from your peace of mind, serenity, honesty, faith and desire to live.
>
> Sincerely, the AIDS virus[9]

So Steve is told that if he changed his thought patterns, the virus would not have power over him. The virus only lives because

Steve has fear; but it would die if Steve had peace of mind, serenity, and the like. The only reality that exists is his own consciousness.

Let's listen to what another AIDS virus says to Karl, who fears he is dying of the disease.

> I don't understand this any better than you do. I don't mean you and your loved ones any harm. I am just trying to exist, just like you, doing it in the best way I know how. Unfortunately, it ends up hurting people. I just want love, just like you do. I am crying out but no one seems to hear me. Maybe if we try listening to each other and talking to each other, we can find a way to exist in peace of mind without hurting each other. Right now, I feel like you only want to destroy me rather than dealing with whatever it is inside of you that brought me here. Please don't hate me and try to destroy me. Love me.
>
> Let's talk and listen to each other and try to live in peace. Thanks.
>
> Signed, AIDS[10]

Let's not hurry over this exercise in positive thinking! AIDS, and the threat of death that it brings, is presented here not as an enemy but simply as a part of the collective human consciousness. Indeed, the virus just wants to be loved, like we all do. It really does not want to hurt Karl, but is crying out for recognition and personal affirmation. Indeed, if Karl and the virus can listen to each other they could "live in peace."

What is more, the virus was attracted to Karl because of his thoughts. The virus counsels him to deal "with whatever it is inside of you that brought me here." In the end, Karl has retained his godhood after all; the virus is there because Karl attracted it by wrong thinking. And evidently it can be expelled by Karl if only he had different thoughts. But we might wonder, does he really want to get rid of it? According to this scenario, maybe he wants to keep it because he feels sorry for the AIDS virus, because after all, the virus is also just looking for love.

The bottom line: Death and disease are illusions from which we must be delivered; we have to reprogram ourselves to think differently and presto, the virus will be no more.

Is all of this good news for Steve and Karl?

If Williamson had been able to give these men reasons to believe that when they died of AIDS they need not fear eternity because their sins were forgiven, that would indeed be good news. But Williamson does not go there; she does not believe that we have to give an account at death, and even if we did, we would have nothing to fear since we are already entirely holy and sin does not exist. She does not give those suffering from AIDS any substantive reason for unrestrained optimism except the notion that positive thoughts in and of themselves have inherent value. And if we just reprogrammed our thoughts, the virus would be under our control; and in any event, we need not fear what doesn't have objective existence.

What do we make of this exercise in positive thinking? I do not deny that there is some power in positive thinking; the little engine that said "I think I can . . . I think I can" had a better chance of making it up the hill than the one who said, "I know I can't, I know I can't." But when the optimistic little engine gets to the top of the hill only to discover that the tracks have been washed out, it doesn't matter how often it says "I think I can." Death, a future heaven and hell—we can wish them all away, but if the Bible is right, our wishing cannot change the reality.

For example, we read in the Scriptures, "And just as it is appointed for man to die once, and after that comes judgment, so Christ, having been offered once to bear the sins of many, will appear a second time, not to deal with sin but to save those who are eagerly waiting for him" (Hebrews 9:27–28). The consistent teaching of the Scriptures is that death and judgment are inevitable. These are not simply illusions within our own minds.

We can try to retreat into the fortress of our minds and tell ourselves that death need not be feared, but we should have a healthy fear of death because we intuitively know that death is not the end of our existence. To ignore the warnings of the Bible is like turning off the alarm when the house is on fire.

JESUS OR SCHUCMAN?

According to Jesus, who knows more about death than the rest of us, many people will someday discover that their "right thinking" could not save them from detailed accountability to God and from eternal judgment. He asked the religious leaders of his day, "You serpents, you brood of vipers, how are you to escape being sentenced to hell?" (Matthew 23:33). Yes, the word *hell* was frequently on Jesus' lips.

This is how Jesus describes the final separation of humanity. Speaking of God the Father, Jesus told His listeners that at the end He will say, "Come, you who are blessed by my Father, inherit the kingdom prepared for you from the foundation of the world" (Matthew 25:34). To others He will say, "Depart from me, you cursed, into the eternal fire prepared for the devil and his angels" (v. 41). And then we have Jesus' summary statement, "And these will go away into eternal punishment, but the righteous into eternal life" (v. 46).

Contrast this with *A Course in Miracles*: Obviously, if we do not really die—if death is an illusion—then there is no judgment to come. The Spirit guide (supposedly Jesus) who directed Helen Schucman to write the course assures us that there is no judgment after death. Just read this:

The Last Judgment is generally thought of as a procedure undertaken by God. Actually, it will be undertaken by my brothers with my help. It is a final healing rather than a meting out of punishment, however much you think that punishment is deserved. Punishment is a concept totally opposed to right-mindedness, and the aim of the last judgment is to restore right-mindedness to you. After this, the ability to choose can be directed rationally. Until this distinction is made, however, the vacillation between free and imprisoned will cannot but continue.[11]

So whom should we believe, Jesus—the Jesus of the New Testament—or the spirit guide who revealed this message to Helen Schucman? I hope you agree that Jesus is more qualified than a spirit guide to tell us what lies on the other side of death and how to prepare for it. The claim of Jesus stands in direct opposition to occultism: "Fear not, I am the first and the last, and the living one. I died, and behold I am alive forevermore, and I have the keys of Death and Hades" (Revelation 1:17–18).

We can almost hear the hiss of the serpent repeat the lie of Eden, "You will not surely die." But a lie it is; a lie that will be eternally exposed.

FROM ILLUSION TO REINCARNATION

In Hinduism, the demonic lie that death does not exist often takes the form of a belief in reincarnation. On a plane I sat next to a woman who lived in Pennsylvania but as a child had visions and dreams of another home in some other part of the country. When she became an adult she visited Vermont and actually saw the home that had been a part of her inner consciousness. She came to believe that she had lived in that house during the 1800s and actually knew the name of the person she had been in her previous existence. This was proof, she said, of reincarnation.

I asked her whether she wanted to hear a biblical explanation for her experience. When she said yes, I explained that the atmosphere was filled with spirits—demonic spirits—and that there could be transmigration of demons, but a not a transmigration of souls. I assured her that she had not lived in that house in a previous generation, but that evil spirits had communicated to her information about that house in Vermont.

She indignantly replied, "I am not into evil spirits—I do communicate with spirits, but I receive only the good ones."

"How do you tell the difference?" I asked.

"It's easy. The good ones are always clothed with light."

Read the literature of Spirituality and you will repeatedly find references to light. In her book *Embraced by the Light*, Betty Eadie gives a fantastic account of her visit to "the other side." She claims to have seen Jesus, engulfed in light, who assured her that there was no judgment. But her Jesus is not the Jesus of the New Testament.

That day on the plane, I shared with the woman sitting next to me the warning of 2 Corinthians 11:13–14, "For such men are false apostles, deceitful workmen, disguising themselves as apostles of Christ. And no wonder, for even Satan disguises himself as an angel of light." Because God is light, Satan always produces his false light to mimic God and assure us that we need not fear judgment. Marianne Williamson retells the Devil's lie that God's love cancels all judgment and then adds, "He cannot think with anger or judgment; He is mercy and compassion and total acceptance."[12]

Really? For a different opinion just read Romans 1:18–32!

A BIBLICAL VIEW OF DEATH

The Bible teaches that we are both a physical and spiritual creation. Looked at in one way, our soul or spirit is more important than our physical body. Indeed, the soul survives the body at death. But the New Testament stresses the coming resurrection when the immaterial aspects of who we are will be united with our body—thus, we are redeemed by Christ, body, soul, and spirit. To say that only our consciousness exists and that the physical world is an illusion is not only false, but detrimental to any honest appraisal of who we are in the world.

The Bible does not encourage us to deny death, but rather to stare at it with all of its horror and finality. Death is seen as universal, for "the soul who sins will die" (Ezekeil 8:4). And, after death comes judgment. No wonder death is seen a thief, as an intruder who takes away everything that we have lived for in this world. "For he must reign until he has put all his enemies under his feet. The last enemy to be destroyed is death" (1 Corinthians 15:25–26).

Nor should we deny sorrow; we are given tear ducts that we might mourn those who have passed from us. Death is almost always accompanied by fear—fear of the unknown, fear of what meeting God will be like, and a universal fear of eternity. This is proof that God has "put eternity into our hearts" (see Ecclesiastes 3:11) and that we know intuitively that life on the earth is not all there is.

Eckhart Tolle is not only wrong but foolish when he says he never thinks of death because only the *now* exists! Yes, only the now exists at this moment, but in ten years there will be a very different *now*. Do we say we shouldn't buy groceries for next week, because all that matters is the *now*? I've known people to spend more time preparing for a trip to Europe than preparing for their death. We should prepare for death not only because it is inevitable, but also because it is the entrance to a whole new world of indescribable bliss or unimaginable horror.

But—and it is time for some good news—death does not have

the last word in the lives of those who believe in Jesus. Listen to His words as He stood at the tomb of Lazarus, "I am the resurrection and the life. Whoever believes in me, though he die, yet shall he live, and everyone who lives and believes in me shall never die" (John 11:25–26).

For those who believe in Jesus, death is a pathway from this life into God's presence.

Remember the words of Hamlet in Shakespeare's play? In a moment of deep contemplation he mused, "To be, or not to be: that is the question" (III. i. 56). He was contemplating suicide because life had become unbearable. Yet when he thought of where that might lead him, he continued,

> Whether 'tis nobler in the mind to suffer
> The slings and arrows of outrageous fortune,
> Or to take arms against a sea of troubles,
> And by opposing end them? To die: to sleep;
> No more; and by a sleep we say we end
> The heart-ache and the thousand natural shocks
> That flesh is heir to, 'tis a consummation
> Devoutly to be wish'd. To die, to sleep;
> To sleep: perchance to dream: ay, there's the rub;
> For in that sleep of death what dreams may come
> When we have shuffled off this mortal coil.
>
> (III. i. 58–67)

Hamlet finds suicide both attractive and repulsive. If he could be sure that it would rid him of his sea of troubles, he would do it; but he fears that "undiscover'd country from whose bourn / No traveller returns " (III. i. 79–80). His present ills might be pleasant in comparison to the fate that would await him.

Compare Hamlet's dilemma with that of Paul:

For to me, to live is Christ and to die is gain. But if I am to live on in the flesh, this will mean fruitful labor for me; and I do not know which to choose. But I am hard-pressed from both directions, having the desire to depart and be with Christ, for that is very much better; yet to remain on in the flesh is more necessary for your sake. (Philippians 1:21–24 NASB)

Hamlet says, "Live or die, I lose!" Paul says, "Live or die, I win!"

WHAT A DIFFERENCE TRUSTING CHRIST MAKES!

DISCUSSION QUESTIONS

1. Read the accounts in Genesis 2:17 and 3:4. What was the contradiction between the serpent's word to Eve (3:4) and God's word to Eve (2:17)? What was the result?

2. How does Eckhart Tolle deal with death? What does Marianne Williamson, in her interpretation of *A Course in Miracles*, say about power over disease? In contrast to their writings, what do we learn about death from the Bible in Hebrews 9:27–28?

3. Helen Schucman writes that there is no death, and therefore also no subsequent judgment. (See Dr. Lutzer's quote from her book on this point.) Contrast that erroneous teaching with the words of Jesus in Matthew 23:33; 25:34, 41. How must we understand Jesus' claim in Revelation 1:17–18?

4. Read the warning of 2 Corinthians 11:13–14. How might we apply the truth of this passage to our discussion of Satan's deception and his disguises of the truth?

5. Dr. Lutzer devotes an entire section in this chapter to the biblical view of death. Discuss his key points. Include in your discussion the texts of 1 Corinthians 15:25–26; John 11:25–26; and Philippians 1:21–24.

Chapter 5

REDEFINING
MORALITY

"LET ME REMEMBER THERE IS NO SIN"
—A Course in Miracles

ADAM AND EVE DESIRED to eat the fruit of the forbidden tree because they were promised that they could be their own God, living by their own rules and determining right versus wrong for themselves. The serpent assured them that they could disregard what God had said and conduct their lives according to their own instincts. God's will could be replaced with their will, and they could do whatever seemed right to them.

Recall that the serpent began by introducing doubt into Eve's mind regarding the clear command of God. "Did God actually say?" (Genesis 3:1). Now that the seed of doubt had been planted, he watered it with the allurement of special knowledge. If she and her husband disobeyed, their "eyes [would] be opened" and they would be like God, "knowing good and evil" (Genesis 3:5). This special knowledge gave them permission to have moral freedom.

Imagine, *they* would know "good and evil"! There was some truth in Satan's promise. After they ate they did know good and evil; but they did not know it as God does, namely, as a surgeon might "know a disease." Adam and Eve now knew good and evil by personal experience; they knew it because they were now a part of the corruption of everything that was holy and good. And because they were finite, incapable of knowing the future, they were ill-equipped to run their own lives—but they would still try.

Adam and Eve introduced us to the notion that our intuitions are reliable and our feelings more infallible than God's commands. They would not only be law*breakers* but become their own law*makers*, doing what they saw as right in their own eyes. Good and evil would now be theirs to determine by intuition and experience. They were the masters of their fate, the captains of their souls.

MEET THE GOD WHO IS US

Now let's put the logic together: We've learned that the New Spirituality says that we are all God; we are already entirely holy; and whatever happens to us takes place because we will it. In such a world, death and sickness cannot exist; hence, they are illusions, a dream from which we must awake.

It follows that there can be no distinction between good and evil. In a world where "all is God and God is all," evil must have the same source and nature as good. And since we are not physical but spiritual beings, in this realm, good and evil as we know it cannot exist. Even crime is an illusion or at least we cannot be blamed for it.

Eckhart Tolle agrees. Listen as he makes the point that we cannot be responsible for our actions since we are neither our bodies nor our thoughts, but our real existence is found only in the parallel spiritual universe he calls consciousness. Note carefully:

> Does this mean that people are not responsible for what they do when they are possessed by the pain-body? My answer is: How can they be? *How can you be responsible when you are unconscious, when you don't know what you are doing?* However, in the greater scheme of things, human beings are meant to evolve into conscious beings, and those who don't will suffer the consequences of their unconsciousness. They are out of line with the evolutionary impulse of the universe.[1] (italics mine)

Now we get to the heart of the matter. We cannot really distinguish good from evil since they both arise from the same life force; added to that is the notion that our outer actions are only illusionary, and you can better grasp why we are not responsible for our actions. To quote Tolle again, "The deeper interconnectedness of all things and events implies that *the mental labels of good and bad are ultimately illusionary.* They always imply a limited perspective and so are true only relatively and temporarily"[2] (italics added).

So there you have it: the mental labels of good and bad are ultimately illusionary. Tolle teaches that we as humans are not born spiritually dead, but spiritually unconscious. Our real self cannot be separated from God because the real self is a part of God. So we must simply affirm who we are as existing in God and deny that evil has any part in our lives. The reason we cannot hold people accountable for what their bodies do is because only the realm of spirit is real.

Tolle adds, "You do not become good by trying to be good, but by finding the goodness that is already in you, and allowing the goodness to emerge. But it can only emerge if something fundamental changes in your state of consciousness."[3] If only we lived in the realm of consciousness, we would find the latent goodness within each of us. So, evil is simply a misunderstanding of our egos; *the fundamental part of us is perfect.*

Marianne Williamson echoes the same notions.

> Only love is real. Nothing else actually exists. If a person behaves unlovingly, then, that means that regardless of their negativity—anger or whatever—their behavior was derived from fear and doesn't actually exist. They're hallucinating. You forgive them, then, because there is nothing to forgive. Forgiveness is discernment between what is real and what is not real.[4]

Imagine! Behavior done from fear doesn't actually exist! You are to forgive those who have wronged you because *there is nothing to forgive*! Since they are perfect just as you are, evil does not exist. This news would hardly be welcomed by those who endured the Holocaust; nor would it be good news to the young woman who was raped here in Chicago this past week. Yes, the New Spirituality teaches that the labels *good* and *evil* are meaningless and only love exists!

Centuries before Oprah's friends advertised their teachings, Buddhism and Hinduism taught that good and evil are only illusions; they only appear to differ from one another. Alan Watts, who is credited with making Zen Buddhism palatable to Americans, explains it this way: "Life is like a play where you see good and bad men in conflict on the stage, but behind the curtain, they are the best of friends. Backstage, God and Satan go hand in hand. Only the uninformed differentiate between good and evil. To quote Yen-Men, one of the great Eastern teachers, 'If you wish the plain truth, be not concerned about right and wrong. The conflict between right and wrong is the sickness of the mind.'"

Charles Manson will not go down in history as a great theologian, but because he had adopted the same pantheistic view of God, the mass murderer asked, "If God is all, what is evil?" His reasoning was clear: good and evil both reside in God. Just so, the New Spirituality teaches that God is male and female; plus and minus; darkness and light; He is perfection and also what is sometimes wrongly called sin. In this universe, everything is good, for everything is God.

Again, Tolle agrees. The reason we think we know the difference between right and wrong is because we are collectively insane. It is a form of madness. He writes,

> Recognize the ego for what it is: a collective dysfunction, the insanity of the human mind. . . . Once you see the ego for what it is, it becomes much easier to remain nonreactive toward it. You don't take it personally anymore. There is no complaining, blaming, accusing, or making wrong. Nobody is wrong. It is the ego in someone, that's all.[5]

Perhaps now we can better understand the exchange that took place between Oprah Winfrey and self-proclaimed Satanist Michael Aquino. More than twenty years ago, on the February 17, 1988, program, Aquino described Satanists as "very decent, very law-abiding people . . . [who] have nothing to do with evil." Oprah was surprised that this was the case, given the gruesome stories connected with Satanism that occasionally surface in the news. But Aquino said that the idea that Satan was evil was a gross misconception that he would "lay at the doorstep of the Christian value system."[6]

Indeed! Looked at in one way, Aquino was right on both counts. First, given the Eastern mind-set, Satanism is not evil—precisely because nothing can be evil. Satan is only God in another form; the dualism we see in the world and as taught in the Bible is just the way things appear to us, but not the way they are "behind the curtain."

Second, please note that Aquino was right in holding Christianity accountable for making moral distinctions; it has the audacity of calling Satanism evil, for example. We plead guilty, of course. The Judeo-Christian worldview can call something evil precisely because it does not believe that everything is God; nor does it teach that individuals are God and therefore they have the right to do as they please. Satan is not God; we are not God but; to the contrary, God is personal and exists independently of His creation.

We've already learned that we need not fear judgment. Here in more detail is Marianne Williamson's assurance that we need never fear God.

> For many people, God is a frightening concept. Asking God for help doesn't seem comforting if we think of Him as something outside ourselves, or capricious or judgmental. But God is love. . . . But God remains who He is and always has been: the energy, the thought of unconditional love. He cannot think with anger or judgment; He is mercy and compassion and total acceptance. The problem is that we have forgotten this, and so we have forgotten who we ourselves are.[7]

Meanwhile, we as Christians are accused of being tied to the elementary distinctions of physical existence. We betray our lack of understanding; we just have not experienced the true nature of reality. If only we were to save ourselves by a transformation of consciousness, we would get beyond such distinctions. Since evil does not exist, it follows that man's problem is not sin but ignorance. All that we need is enlightenment.

Many decent people who have been lured into the New Spirituality because of its use of Christian terminology have no idea of the consequences of believing that we are all a part of the force called God. Nor do they realize that these teachings affirm that evil does not have actual existence, and humans cannot be held responsible for what we erroneously call evil.

The New Spirituality with its denial of morality is actually more dangerous than the secular humanism we have all heard so much about. Inconsistent as the humanists are, they still wish to cling to some of the standards of the Judeo-Christian tradition. Atheism still teaches the need for morality of some sort. But the New Spirituality logically abolishes morality altogether.

WHY DOES THIS HAPPEN TO ME?

Even though evil is an illusion and, strictly speaking, does not exist, the fact is that we have terrible things that happen to us. At least before we experience a transformation of consciousness, we experience grief in what Tolle calls "the pain body." How do we account for this? The answer: Since we are God, it cannot happen to us unless we will it. In other words, we attract it to us because of our thoughts. We cause whatever grief comes our way.

Remember Marianne Williamson saying that Karl "willed" the AIDS virus? The reasoning behind it is clear: We are God, evil in reality does not exist, the Universe is perfect, and therefore nothing terrible really happens; but if something that might be called terrible does happen to you, it is because you, as God, willed it.

Listen to Rhonda Byrne's explanation for those times in history when masses of lives were lost. People wonder, she says, how victims of, for example, the Holocaust or calamitous natural disasters, could have attracted such events. Byrne contends that the victims' persistent thoughts attract them to being in the wrong place at the wrong time.

Read this carefully:

> By the law of attraction, they had to be on the same frequency as the event. It doesn't necessarily mean that they thought of the exact event, but the frequency of their thoughts matched the frequency of the event. If people believe they can be in the wrong place at the wrong time, and they have no control over outside circumstances, those thoughts of fear, separation, and powerlessness, if persistent can attract them to being at the wrong place at the wrong time.[8]

She urges us to believe and know that our life experiences are in our hands, and only good can come out of our life if we think correctly. "You have a choice," she says, and "whatever you think *will* become your life experience."

This is standard fare in occult religion. Years ago, a graduate of *est* (Erhard Seminar Training) stated that she listened for two hours while two women therapists explained how the Jews must have "wanted" to be burned by the Germans, and that those who starve in the Sahara Desert must want it to happen. When asked what can be done about a child starving in the desert, one of the therapists snapped angrily, "What can I do if a child is determined to starve?"[9] Erhard, like the New Spirituality teachers, believed the universe was perfect, and that we are God in the universe, and we *caused* any evil that might exist.

Byrne concurs. She says that this is a friendly universe. We should proclaim, "This is a magnificent Universe. The Universe is bringing all good things to me. The Universe is conspiring for me in all things. The Universe is supporting me in everything I do. The Universe meets all of my needs immediately."[10] And again, "You are the creator and there is an easy way to create by using the law of attraction."[11]

In fact, we never have to lack benefits in this world because of the law of attraction.

> It's like having the Universe as your catalogue. You flip through it and say, "I'd like to have this experience and I'd like to have that product and I'd like to have a person like that." It is you placing your order with the Universe. It's really that easy.[12]

Indeed, if you are overweight, it is because you have been thinking fat thoughts.[13]

In passing, this explains why I should never have to feel guilty for the way I treat you. Betrayal, theft, or personal injury should not fill me with regret. Whatever has happened to you, happened because you, as God, willed it. You attracted my evil because of your thoughts. No need for me to apologize in a perfect Universe. To quote *A Course in Miracles*, "The end of guilt will never come as long as you believe there is a reason for it. For you must learn that guilt is always totally insane, and has no reason."[14]

In a perfect world where evil is an illusion, guilt is a sickness of the mind.

THE WARNINGS OF SCRIPTURE

Space forbids a detailed analysis of the moral inconsistencies of pantheism. The fact is that because all mankind is created in the image of God, it is impossible to live without moral values. Regardless of what people say about the illusionary character of evil, no one can live that way. That's why the New Age Movement in America continues to talk about morality. Indeed, it appeals to some noble ideals. Adherents assure us they are working for the betterment of the human race. Such claims, of course, are in direct contradiction with the philosophical base of New Age thought that says good and evil are only a sickness of the mind.

The image of the New Spirituality is that of a benevolent worldview, interested in the harmony of mankind with peace and justice for all. We are told that the techniques used to plug into the spiritual forces of the Universe exist solely for the development of mankind and the exploration of his latent potential. Who can quarrel with such lofty ideals?

But these beautiful platitudes are no different than the seductive tree that Eve could not resist. She did not realize that there is an ugly side to Satan's lofty promise that she and Adam could run their own lives. Just so, behind the mask of peace and love, there lies the complete destruction of morality. It represents a much more serious attack on morality than the pragmatism of rationalism. Of necessity, it is the most cruel and barbaric worldview that one can imagine. Imagine a worldview that does not permit us to say that Hitler and Stalin were evil! A worldview where no one should feel guilt!

This is nothing less than fighting against God; this is the satanic lie taken to its most dastardly conclusion. False prophets who call evil good and good evil have always existed. Speaking of such prophets and the people who are anxious to hear their visions and teachings, Isaiah writes:

> For they are a rebellious people, lying children, children unwilling to hear the instruction of the Lord; who say to the seers, "Do not see," and to the prophets, "Do not prophesy to us what is right; speak to us smooth things, prophesy illusions, leave the way, turn aside from the path, let us hear no more about the Holy One of Israel." (Isaiah 30:9–11)

Of such, God says,

> You felt secure in your wickedness, you said, "No one sees me"; your wisdom and your knowledge led you astray, and you said in your heart, "I am, and there is no one besides me." But evil shall come upon you, which you will not know how to charm away; disaster will fall upon you, for which you shall not be able to atone; and ruin shall come upon you suddenly, of which you know nothing. (Isaiah 47:10–11)

Interestingly, after Helen Schucman, the author of *A Course in Miracles*, died, her psychologist later wrote these words, "This woman who had written so eloquently that suffering really did not exist spent the last two years of her life in the blackest psychotic depression I have ever witnessed."[15]

Imagine! She suffered for two years with the "blackest psychotic depression"; yet this is the woman who taught others to say, "My sinlessness ensures me perfect peace, eternal safety, everlasting love, freedom forever from all thought of loss; complete deliverance from suffering" (Lesson #337). Clearly, saying it is so does not make it so!

"Woe to those who call evil good, and good evil; who substitute darkness for light and light for darkness" (Isaiah 5:20 NASB).

How can educated people be convinced of the absurdities of the New Spirituality? In the next chapter we will learn about the coming of the Antichrist and discover that God not only allows people to believe what they yearn to, but judges them by blinding their minds to the truth.

THOSE WHO BELIEVE THESE LIES
DO SO AT THEIR OWN PERIL.

DISCUSSION QUESTIONS

1. In the garden of Eden, what did the serpent do to deceive Adam and Eve into redefining morality for themselves? What lessons can we take from the opening discussion regarding Adam and Eve and moral freedom?

2. Discuss the logic of the New Spirituality that suggests that we all exist in God and we are already entirely holy.

3. Describe Eckhart Tolle's and Marianne Williamson's notion that we need not fear judgment for our actions. According to Tolle, "the mental labels of good and bad are ultimately illusionary." As a society and as individuals, can we accept the notion that crime and evil are simply an illusion? How can atrocities such as the Holocaust be reconciled to this logic?

4. How does New Age Spirituality thinking view the nature of God? Contrast that view with the Judeo-Christian view of God's nature.

5. How do these New Spirituality authors explain the pain, suffering, and grief that happen in our lives? How does Rhonda Byrne's "law of attraction" come into play here?

6. Scripture gives strong warnings about false prophets who call evil good and good evil. Discuss Isaiah 30:9–11 and Isaiah 47:10–11 and their application to false prophets.

7. Read 2 Timothy 4:3. In light of this verse, what is the basis for the teachings of the New Spirituality examined in the preceding chapters? Do they reflect a divine or human origin and orientation?

Chapter Six

THE LIE AND
THE END TIMES

"MIRACLES ENABLE YOU TO HEAL THE SICK
AND RAISE THE DEAD BECAUSE YOU MADE
SICKNESS AND DEATH YOURSELF,
AND CAN THEREFORE ABOLISH BOTH"
—*A Course in Miracles*

IN THE HOFBERG LIBRARY in Vienna, Austria, there is a spear believed by many to be the one used to pierce the side of Christ. One day when Adolf Hitler was in his early twenties, he overheard a tour guide point out the spear to a group of guests and say, "This spear is shrouded in mystery; whoever unlocks its secrets will rule the world." Later Hitler said that those words had changed his whole life.[1]

Hitler, you will recall, spent four years in Vienna, living in flophouses and drawing sketches to earn enough money to stay alive. He spent all of his free time in the Hofberg Library, reading books on history and the occult. He became an expert in Eastern religions and was known to purchase such books in used bookstores and then resell them so that he could buy more.

After hearing the comment about the mystery of that spear, Hitler became fascinated with it. He read all he could about its history, trying to determine whether it could, indeed, be traced back to the time of Christ. He soon discovered that there were many spears that vied for the dubious honor of being the one used to smite Christ's side. Nevertheless, he became convinced that this one did have awesome powers for good or evil. He traced it back to the time of Constantine and believed that the emperor had had it in hand when he conquered Rome in AD 312.

In all, Hitler believed that forty-five different Roman emperors or kings had used the spear. He noted that when they had it in their possession they were victorious; when it fell from their sphere of ownership, their empires crumbled, sometimes within a single day.

Young Hitler was mesmerized by this object. He stood staring at it for hours, inviting its hidden powers to invade his soul. He believed this ancient weapon was a bridge between the world of sense and the world of the spirit. He felt as though he himself had held it in his hands in an earlier century. He was bewitched by its mysteries and power. Dr. Walter Johannes Stein, who knew Hitler in those days, says that Hitler was so captivated by the spear that he almost experienced a "total eclipse of self-consciousness" while standing before it.[2]

When Hitler left Vienna to go to Munich, he soon surrounded himself with those who were dedicated to the pursuit of occult experiences and phenomena. The original members of the National Socialist Party (dubbed "the Nazis") were hard-core Satanists who introduced him to deeper levels of "spiritual perception."

Hitler's chief mentor was Dietrich Eckart, who, through the rituals of black magic, enabled Hitler to be transformed into a totally demonized being. Eckart claimed that he had received a satanic annunciation that he was destined to prepare the vessel of the Antichrist, the man who would be inspired by Lucifer to conquer the world and lead the Aryan race to glory.[3]

Young Adolf assumed the uncontested leadership of the Nazi party in 1921, the year he celebrated his thirty-third birthday—the same age at which Christ began His official career. By now he had been taken through deep levels of occult transformation. Like the Antichrist to come, he was completely possessed by evil powers.

Rauschning, who was at one time one of Hitler's associates but later defected to the West and became an adviser to Churchill, observed, "One cannot help but think of him as a medium. Beyond any doubt Hitler was possessed by forces outside of himself, of which the individual Hitler was only the temporary vehicle."[4]

THE CRY FOR A WORLD LEADER

Hitler was, I believe, a prototype of the Antichrist. Prior to the Second World War, Germany was in a state of hyperinflation, so that most Germans had their savings wiped out in a matter of days. Hitler appeared to be a political genius because he brought them out of economic chaos. He was a man who initially gave a sense of pride and identity to the German people, who needed their faith in humanity revived.

Antichrist, I believe, will do the same, but on a worldwide scale. This man will walk onto the stage of history and perform economic and political miracles. He will capture the imagination of millions—billions, rather—who will follow his peace and prosperity platform. With smooth words and reasonable assurances of good intent, he will lure an unsuspecting world into the greatest bloodbath that has ever taken place.

Author Reinhold Kerstan, who witnessed Hitler's rise to power, believes that the world is looking for a leader who will point the way out of economic decline and uncertainty. He says that this generation is open to "an updated Fuehrer."

As the world wonders at the political realignments taking place in Europe, equally significant changes are taking place on the religious map. People are beginning to believe in the very doctrines that Antichrist will proclaim. A religious revolution is taking place that will make the spiritual aspects of Antichrist's rule welcomed by the world.

Hitler had the two characteristics that I believe Antichrist shall someday have: first, awesome demonic control, and second, an intense hatred for the Jews. Just as Hitler intended to exterminate the Jews, Antichrist will eventually try to do the same—but will be prevented from doing so for a reason that will become clear in just a moment.

THE PREDICTIONS OF END TIMES

What kind of doctrines will be taught in the last days? In Matthew 24, Jesus on the Mount of Olives was asked by His disciples when the end times would arrive and what would be the sign of His coming. He answered, "See that no one leads you astray. For many will come in my name, saying, 'I am the Christ,' and they will lead many astray" (v. 4–5). Then a few verses later He adds, "Then if anyone says to you, 'Look, here is the Christ!' or 'There he is!' do not believe it. For false christs and false prophets will arise and perform great signs and wonders, so as to lead astray, if possible, even the elect" (vv. 23–24).

It is not ours to say whether we are in the end times. Previous generations have all believed that Christ was coming in their day, but they obviously were mistaken. So let's not presume to know that we are living in the last days. However, we should certainly note that the political and religious landscape seems to approximate what Jesus predicted.

Jesus said that there would be many christs before His return. We've already noted that in *A Course in Miracles*, we read, "The name of Jesus Christ is but a symbol. It stands for the love that is not of this world. It is a symbol that is safely used as a replacement for the many names of the gods to which you pray."[5] So the name of Jesus is emptied of its meaning so that there can be many "christs" or those who claim that they are just as divine as He was.

When Marianne Williamson was asked, "Was Jesus the only son of God?" she replied in an interview, "Hogwash. First of all, I believe we are all sons of God and our destiny is to be like Jesus. Second, there's only one soul. To say that there is only one begotten son doesn't mean that someone else was it and we are not. It means we are all it. There's only one of us here."[6]

Eckhart Tolle says that Jesus is the picture of every man and every woman on the cross, and then says, "Jesus speaks of the innermost I AM, the essence identity of every man, every woman and every life form, in fact."[7] Again, we have the name of Jesus pressed into service to apply to others, even ourselves. Each of us is Jesus.

Like in Old Testament times, false prophets can be identified because they teach that God need not be feared and there is no final judgment. Listen to God's commentary on them, "The prophets are prophesying lies in my name. I did not send them, nor did I command them or speak to them. They are prophesying to you a lying vision, worthless divination, and the deceit of their own minds" (Jeremiah 14:14). This is an apt description of those who claim to speak on behalf of God today, but are basing their conclusions on their own hunches or intuition.

Today's teachers who claim revelation from the netherworld fall into the same category as ancient prophets who told their people what they wanted to hear. Again God speaks through Jeremiah, "An appalling and horrible thing has happened in the land; the prophets prophey falsely, and the priests rule at their direction; my people love to have it so, but what will you do when the end comes?" (5:30–31) Yes, even today the people—in some instances even *God's* people—love to have it so.

We've previously quoted Paul, "For the time is coming when people will not endure sound teaching, but having itching ears they will accumulate for themselves teachers to suit their own passions, and will turn away from listening to the truth and wander off into myths" (2 Timothy 4:3–4). Those "itching ears" want to hear about a God they need not fear; they want to hear theories that will enable them to exalt themselves. They want doctrine redefined so that they can be comfortable with their personal ambitions and sins.

THE COMING GREAT TRIBULATION

Many of us believe that the return of Christ will take place in two stages. First, there will be the rapture of the church; that is, the catching away of all believers who will be gathered together to be with the Lord. When Paul began the church in Thessalonica, he taught them to look forward to this dramatic event when Jesus returns and the dead saints will be resurrected, and the living saints will be snatched up to meet the Lord in the air (1 Thessalonians 4:13–18). Following this, Antichrist will arise on earth and the great tribulation will ensue. This is followed by the second stage of Christ's return: He will appear with worldwide glory and power to establish His kingdom (see Matthew 24:25–31).

But the dear saints in Thessalonica were experiencing so much persecution that they thought they were already in the great tribulation! So in his second letter to them, Paul clarifies that they can't be in the tribulation because three other events had to take place before this time of suffering came to planet Earth. Let's read his words, "Now concerning the coming of our Lord Jesus Christ and our being gathered together to him, we ask you, brothers, not to be quickly shaken in mind or alarmed, either by a spirit or a spoken word, or a letter seeming to be from us, to the effect that the day of the Lord has come" (2 Thessalonians 2:1–2). The day of the Lord is that period of time when God begins to wrap up history as we know it. Someone in the church at Thessalonica was falsely teaching that the day of the Lord had already come and the church was now in the tribulation.

Paul says that the day of the Lord could not have come yet for several reasons. One, a worldwide apostasy had to come first: "Let no one deceive you in any way. For that day will not come, unless the rebellion comes first" (2 Thessalonians 2:3). Paul says there will be a worldwide rebellion that will come to this earth. The Greek word is "the apostasy"; that is, a falling away from the faith and the acceptance of heresy. What will be taught during this special period of time when people are deluded by false teaching? Elsewhere Paul gives us a hint, or more than a hint, actually. "Now the Spirit expressly says that in later times some will depart from the faith by devoting themselves to deceitful spirits and teachings of demons, through the insincerity of liars whose consciences are seared" (1 Timothy 4:1–2).

The doctrines of the last times will be taught by people who have two identifiable characteristics. First, they will be devoted to deceitful spirits; second, they are people who are insincere liars whose consciences are "seared." We've already learned that the New Spirituality finds its source in the doctrine of demons, but from Paul we learn that those who teach these ideas know better; they are teaching doctrines that are contrary to their own consciences. These teachers have to suppress the truth and put a lid on what their own reason and intuition tell them.

Let us review some of the teachings of *A Course in Miracles*. Surely no one could possibly teach these blasphemies unless they had deadened their conscience.

Lesson #35, "My mind is part of God's. I am very holy."
Lesson #37, "My holiness blesses the world."
Lesson #38, "There is nothing my holiness cannot do."
Lesson #70, "My salvation comes from me."
Lesson #186, "Salvation of the world depends on me."

Intuitively, we know that we are not holy; we know very well that our holiness does not bless the world. To say such foolishness we have to turn from what we know about ourselves and teach obvious lies that exalt us. Why would anyone knowingly teach such deceptions? Because these teachers desperately want these doctrines to be true! To believe the opposite—that we are sinners who need to be redeemed—is simply unthinkable.

Consider this: There may be many people in hell who want to be there. That might sound strange to say; after all, who wants to go to hell? But for some, they would rather choose hell if their only alternative is to admit that Jesus is the only way to God, and that they are terrible sinners who need to be redeemed. We think, for example, of those in the book of Revelation, who though they were tormented, still refused to repent of their love of sin. "The rest of mankind, who were not killed by these plagues, did not repent of the works of their hands nor give up worshiping demons and idols of gold and silver and bronze and stone and wood, which cannot see or hear or walk, nor did they repent of their murders or their sorceries or their sexual immorality or their thefts" (Revelation 9:20–21). Imagine! They are in torment, but will not repent of worshiping demons and sorceries!

So, the first reason Paul says the church couldn't be in the tribulation is because the worldwide apostasy has not yet come. Perhaps the false teachers of our day are preparing the way. Thanks to television and the Internet, these men and women are spreading their heresies around the world.

Second, Paul says the tribulation can't come until the restrainer is taken away. "For the mystery of lawlessness is already at work. Only he who now restrains it will do so until he is out of the way" (2 Thessalonians 2:7). This must be a reference to the ministry of the Holy Spirit through the church. If so, this is another reason why we believe that the church will be raptured before the tribulation. Only when the church is taken out of the world will the influence of the Holy Spirit through God's people be gone. Then all wickedness breaks loose, and the unrestrained evil of the human heart is revealed as the tribulation comes upon the whole world.

Third, Paul says that if the tribulation had already arrived, Antichrist would have appeared. "And then the lawless one will be revealed, whom the Lord Jesus will kill with the breath of his mouth and bring to nothing by the appearance of his coming" (2 Thessalonians 2:8). Only after Antichrist has come will the tribulation come on the earth that will set the stage for the second phase of Christ's appearing. Then when Jesus comes in glory, the Antichrist and all who side with him will be justly destroyed.

THE UNFOLDING EVENTS

Here is the order of events as best I can understand it:

First of all, Antichrist will arise in Europe and speak peace, but he will be preparing for war. The world will be clamoring, "We're so tired of war. Give us the peace candidate!" Antichrist will comply. He will sign a covenant of peace with Israel, and the world will believe that the elusive quest for peace has been achieved.

Second, he will desire global worship and receive it. Read this astounding description of his power,

> And the beast was given a mouth uttering haughty and blasphemous words, and it was allowed to exercise authority for forty-two months. It opened its mouth to utter blasphemies against God, blaspheming his name and his dwelling, that is, those who dwell in heaven. Also it was allowed to make war on the saints and to conquer them. And authority was given it over every tribe and people and language and nation, and all who dwell on earth will worship it, everyone whose name has not been written before the foundation of the world in the book of life of the Lamb who was slain. (Revelation 13:5–8)

For a brief time, Satan's chosen man rules. He breaks the covenant he made with Israel and then will go into the temple of God, and he "takes his seat in the temple of God, proclaiming himself to be God" (2 Thessalonians 2:4). This is one reason why some of us believe that the temple in Jerusalem still has to be rebuilt. For a time Antichrist receives global worship.

Then Paul follows with this description of Antichrist. "The coming of the lawless one is by the activity of Satan with all power and false signs and wonders, and with all wicked deception for those who are perishing, because they refused to love the truth and so be saved" (2 Thessalonians 2:9–10). Then he adds, "Therefore God sends them [the followers of Antichrist] a strong delusion, so that they may be believe what is false, in order that all may be condemned who did not believe the truth but had pleasure in unrighteousness" (vv. 11–12).

The Antichrist will display Satan's power with false signs and wonders! Twice in the New Testament these descriptions, namely, "power and false signs and wonders," are used to refer to the miracles of Jesus. Again we see how Satan mimics the miracles of Jesus. And the world will believe him! God will send them spiritual blindness so that they will believe these miracles and think that at last they have a ruler who understands the nature of Spirituality and is able to tap into the great powers of the Universe.

When Paul says, "Therefore God sends them a strong delusion, so that they may believe what is false" (v. 11), the Greek text literally says that people will believe *"The Lie,"* namely, that a man can be worshiped as God. Whether it was a Roman emperor demanding worship because he was divine, or whether it is the *Course in Miracles* telling us that we are all divine, the delight to the Prince of Darkness is overwhelming when man attempts to take God's place.

It is sobering to realize that God gives people what they want—that is, spiritual blindness so that they believe in the divinity of Antichrist and, for that matter, in their own divinity. The audacity to believe the absurd notion that man can usurp the prerogatives of God—the ability to believe such nonsense is a judgment of God. And although Paul says that the delusion that God sends is still future, I can't help but believe that such delusions are already rampant in our culture.

As we have learned, when *A Course in Miracles* is taught, the students arrive at Lesson #191, which reads, "I am the holy Son of God Himself." And then comes the assurance these are the words you should say if you want to undo hell. To quote, "I am the holy Son of God Himself. I cannot suffer, I cannot be in pain; I cannot suffer loss, nor fail to do all that salvation asks"; and then we read, "When you say this, a miracle has lighted up all the dark and ancient caverns."[8] Furthermore, we are assured that when we say this, all illusions come to an end.

Be advised that what some of us would call the mother of all illusions is touted in New Age literature as the *end* of all illusions! Yes, perhaps the delusion promised by Paul has already begun, and this might in part account for the success of the false teachers I've attempted to expose in this book. God gives those who want to believe in the divinity of man special spiritual blindness so that they can do so with confidence and without conscience.

THE RETURN OF JESUS

Antichrist rules for a short period of time, and in the battle of Armageddon, he turns against the Jews, intending to exterminate them. The armies of the world press toward Israel, and all the nations of the earth choose sides. And then this conflict is severely interrupted. Jesus Christ returns in glory.

The Old Testament prophet Zechariah described it this way: "Then the Lord will go out and fight against those nations as when he fights on a day of battle. On that day his feet shall stand on the Mount of Olives that lies before Jerusalem on the east, and the Mount of Olives shall be split in two from east to west by a very wide valley, so that one half of the Mount shall move northward, and the other half southward" (Zechariah 14:3–4). Jesus then defends Jerusalem and is acknowledged as King.

Jesus previews His own coming with this picture:

For as the lightning comes from the east and shines as far as the west, so will be the coming of the Son of Man. . . . Immediately after the tribulation of those days the sun will be darkened, and the moon will not give its light, and the stars will fall from heaven, and the powers of the heavens will be shaken. Then will appear in heaven the sign of the Son of Man, and then all the tribes of the earth will mourn, and they will see the

Son of Man coming on the clouds of heaven with power and great glory. (Matthew 24:27, 29–30)

Paul says: "The Lord Jesus [will be] revealed from heaven with his mighty angels in flaming fire, inflicting vengeance on those who do not know God and on those who do not obey the gospel of our Lord Jesus. They will suffer the punishment of eternal destruction, away from the presence of the Lord and from the glory of his might" (2 Thessalonians 1:7–9). Later he gives this detail: "The Lord Jesus will kill [Antichrist] with the breath of his mouth" (2 Thessalonians 2:8).

Personally, I like the description in the book of Revelation the best. As you read this, remember that those who are arrayed in fine linen are believers in Jesus who will have been previously raptured to return with Jesus.

Then I saw heaven opened, and behold, the white horse! The one sitting on it is called Faithful and True, and in righteousness he judges and makes war. His eyes are like a flame of fire, and on his head are many diadems, and he has a name written that no one knows but himself. He is clothed in a robe dipped in blood, and the name by which he is called is The Word of God. And the armies of heaven, arrayed in fine linen, white and pure, were following him on white horses. From his mouth comes a sharp sword with which to strike down the nations, and he will rule them with a rod of iron. He will tread the winepress of the fury of the wrath of God the Almighty. On his robe and on his thigh he has a name written, King of kings, and Lord of lords." (Revelation 19:11–16)

And thus "the lie" comes to an inglorious end. Satan's deceptions are unmasked and Jesus Christ is exalted. Teachers such as Eckhart Tolle and others like him are exposed as frauds. Vain words are revealed for what they are. And the truth is both proclaimed and believed.

"Now the salvation and the power and the kingdom of our God and the authority of his Christ have come, for the accuser of our brothers has been thrown down, who accuses them day and night before our God. And they have conquered him by the blood of the Lamb and by the word of their testimony, for they loved not their lives even unto death."
(Revelation 12:10–11)

DISCUSSION QUESTIONS

1. Review Dr. Lutzer's discussion of Adolf Hitler's obsession with the occult. How extensive was his obsession, and to what extent did it control him? For what reasons does Dr. Lutzer believe Hitler is a prototype of the Antichrist?

2. Who is the Antichrist, and what will he try to accomplish during the end times? Is the world political scene ripe today for his appearance?

3. Read Matthew 24:4, 23. What do these verses predict? How do the writings of Marianne Williamson and Eckhart Tolle fall in line with these predictions? (See also Jeremiah 14:14 and 2 Timothy 4:3–4.)

4. Dr. Lutzer emphasizes three key events of the end times. Discuss these events and their associated Scripture passages: the rapture (1 Thessalonians 4:13–18), the great tribulation (2 Thessalonians 2:1–2), and Christ's return to reign (Matthew 24:25–31). What will characterize the great tribulation? (See 2 Thessalonians 2:3.)

5. Read 1 Timothy 4:1–2. The false doctrines of the last times will be taught by people who have two identifiable characteristics. Discuss those characteristics and what those people will try to do during the end times.

6. Dr. Lutzer provides three reasons why the church cannot currently be in the tribulation. Discuss these three reasons and what the Bible teaches about them. (See 2 Thessalonians 2:3; 2 Thessalonians 2:7; and 2 Thessalonians 2:8.)

7. This chapter offers a section on the unfolding of end-time events. Discuss these events in their chronological order while applying the associated Scripture passages.

8. Read Matthew 24:27–30, a passage dealing with Jesus' glorious return. (See also Revelation 19:11–16.) What will become of Satan's delusions?

THE NEED
OF THE HOUR

WHAT SHOULD WE be doing in this age of growing spiritual interest amid growing spiritual confusion? Do we simply stand by, cursing the darkness, or do we make a difference and light a candle where God has planted us?

I deeply believe that we have a great opportunity to make an impact on our culture, and more important, to change the spiritual direction of those who are within our sphere of influence. Think of the privilege of living at a time when we have millions of seekers trying to find their way amid a blizzard of religious options. If we are sensitive to human need we will soon learn that many people are seeking fulfillment—and we have the privilege of helping them on their spiritual journey.

I'm convinced that if our nation turns to God, it will not be because of a great nationwide campaign; it will not be because we have made use of the Internet, religious movies, or more television programs. If we see a national revival of Christianity, it will be because individual Christians stepped to the plate and shared their faith, living out the gospel in their homes, neighborhoods, and working environments.

Our present challenge is like that of the early Christians who lived in a culture driven by a passionate commitment to spirituality. Emperor worship, along with a myriad of gods and goddesses, dominated Roman culture and thought. The pagans were willing to add Jesus to the long list of gods that could be worshiped, but what they could not tolerate is the idea that there was only one true God who declared that all other rivals were worthless idols. In other words, Jesus could be a god, but what offended the pagans was the Christian teaching that He was "King of kings and Lord of lords."

In the midst of such a pluralistic culture, the apostle Peter wrote, "But even if you should suffer for righteousness' sake, you will be blessed. Have no fear of them, nor be troubled, but in your hearts honor Christ the Lord as holy, always being prepared to make a defense to anyone who asks you for a reason for the hope that is in you; yet do it with gentleness and respect, having a good conscience, so that, when you are slandered, those who revile your good behavior in Christ may be put to shame" (1 Peter 3:14–16).

Have no fear! Defend Christ with gentleness and respect! Live with a good conscience! These words are as relevant to us as they were in the first century. Yes, we must challenge the religious climate of our time, but we must do it with humility, respect, and armed with knowledge so that we are always prepared to give a reason for the hope within us.

So how do we witness to our faith?

SILENT NO MORE

Recently, I spoke to a pastor who lives in east Germany, the area that was until 1989 under Soviet control. He explained how communism taught the Christians to be silent about their beliefs. Those who professed faith and attended church were marginalized by intimidation and humiliation. A parent might be told, "I understand you attend church . . . well, unless you stop attending, your children will not be allowed to attend school, and you will be bypassed for a job promotion." Through such pressure, the Christians became silent, their faith was privatized, and not passed on to the next generation. Sadly, even now, only about 13 percent of the population attends church.

Today, there are leaders in Washington who believe that Christians are the enemy and must be silenced. The separation of church and state is interpreted to mean that all expressions of Christianity in the "public square" should be criminalized. Equally ominous is the cultural notion that we are hateful if we suggest that Jesus is the only way to God and if we affirm that other religions hold out false hopes and promises. People would not mind if Oprah were to testify of her faith in Christ; but if she were to say that Christ is the only way to God, a storm of criticism would erupt. And yet, unless we understand why Christ is the only way, we have not understood the gospel.

Let us agree that we will be silent no more. We must avoid being obnoxious, but at the same time we also must avoid keeping our mouths closed. I've discovered the best way to share my faith is by asking questions, trying to find out where others are on their own spiritual journey. We must invite discussion and understand what others are thinking about God, religion, and Jesus in particular. How is this done?

Here are some questions I've often used to begin a spiritual conversation:

- Where are you on your spiritual journey?
- How much adult consideration have you given to the Bible?
- How do you understand the idea of God?
- What has been your experience, if any, with Christianity?
- Would you mind if I were to share with you something that someone once shared with me that changed my life?
- I'd love to pray for you; do you have anything you'd like me to pray about in the next couple of weeks?

Of course, there are other questions that would be helpful. But we never want to give a discourse about Christ without first kindly learning where people are at on the spiritual spectrum. We simply have to return to the practice of Jesus in the Gospels, who dialogued with those around Him by asking questions.

Many Christians are intimidated when sharing their faith because they think they need to know all the answers. If the truth be told, becoming a good listener is more important than becoming a good talker in our religious climate. People want to be heard. And listening to both what they say and what they feel is the first step to building a bridge that leads to their own hearts.

If you encounter hostility, befriend the person to learn why they are so angry or why they have been turned off by Christianity. Many have, humanly speaking, good reason to regard us with skepticism and distrust. Friendship—true friendship—is still the best means of evangelism. One reason why the early church was so successful is that they practiced the art of hospitality. Their kindness reached the world.

I've often given a friend or colleague a book to read that I think they'll enjoy and then told them that I'd like to discuss it with them in the next few weeks. The book itself might or might not be gospel centered; what I want to do initially is to open up dialogue. Other books can follow.

GOD'S PART AND OURS

Those who are into Spirituality are often very open to talking about spiritual matters. Sometimes they want to share what they have learned; or they want to challenge traditional beliefs. You might be pleasantly surprised by how ready your friends and colleagues are to discuss these ideas. Many have read Eckhart Tolle, or know something about the Course in Miracles.

Be patient. Be kind.

Those who buy into the New Spirituality are often the most difficult to reach with the gospel for two reasons: First, they are convinced that they already have enlightenment; they are the privileged ones who have discovered God in the depths of their soul. For them, to be told that they must seek God through Christ alone is an affront to their sense of inclusiveness that tells them that there must be many ways to the divine.

Second, as we have learned in this book, many are actually blinded by Satan, who has given them the kind of spiritual experience they believe to be authentic. When Jesus told the parable about the sower, some of the grain fell on a hard path, and He explained, "The ones along the path are those who have heard; then the devil comes and takes away the word from their hearts, so that they may not believe and be saved" (Luke 8:12).

This is why our witness must always be done with helpless dependence on God. We must be reminded that only God can open the human heart and draw sinners to Himself. Our responsibility is to share the faith; it is God's responsibility to supply the enablement to respond to the knowledge that has been imparted. As Jesus put it, "No one can come to me unless the Father who sent me draws him. And I will raise him up on the last day" (John 6:44).

God will not hold us accountable if others do not believe the gospel; He will hold us accountable if we do not share the gospel with others. Our responsibility is to sow the seed, but only He can prepare the soil of the human heart to receive it. Only He can grant the faith needed to believe the gospel.

As Paul wrote, "I planted, Apollos watered, but God gave the growth" (1 Corinthians 3:6). Witnessing to our faith in Christ is the great need of the hour!

NOTES

Welcome to the World of Spirituality

1. Martha Sherrill, "Welcome to the Banquet," *O Magazine*, May 2008, 280.

2. Ibid., 281.

Chapter 1: Meet Oprah and Her Friends

1. "The Church of Oprah Exposed," You Tube, http://www.youtube.com/watch?v=JW4LLwkgmqA (accessed on August 29,2008).

2. A New Earth Online Class, Chapter 1 Transcript, www.oprah.com.

3. Ann Oldenburg, "The Divine Miss Winfrey?" *USA Today*, May 11, 2006, Life section.

4. Kathryn Lofton, professor at Reed College, quoted in ibid.

5. Cathleen Falsani, "There's No Denying the Power of Oprah," *Chicago Sun-Times*, November 18, 2005.

6. Marcia Nelson, *The Gospel According to Oprah* (Louisville: Westminster John Knox, 2005), 57.

7. Quoted in Carrington Steele, *Don't Drink the Kool-Aid: Oprah, Obama and the Occult* (Scotts Valley, CA: CreateSpace, 2008), 39.

8. Ibid., 45.

9. Rhonda Byrne, *The Secret* (New York: Atria Books, 2005), 43.

10. Ibid., xi.

11. Steele, 27.

12. Helen Schucman, *A Course in Miracles: Text, Workbook for Students, Manual for Teachers* (Glen Ellen, CA: The Foundation for Inner Peace, 1977), ix.

13. Marianne Williamson, *The Gift of Change* (San Francisco: HarperCollins, 2004), 244.

14. C. S. Lewis, *Mere Christianity* (San Francisco: HarperCollins, 2001), 28.

Chapter 2: Redefining God

1. Paul Tripp, *A Quest for More* (Greensboro, NC: New Growth Press, 2007), 29.

2. Helen Schucman, *A Course in Miracles: Text, Workbook for Students, Manual for Teachers* (Glen Ellen, CA: The Foundation for Inner Peace, 1977), Workbook for Students, 53.

3. Carl Sagan, *Cosmos* (New York: Ballantine, 1985), 1.

4. Schucman, Workbook for Students, 363.

5. Ibid., 119.

6. Ibid., 351.

7. Ibid., 102.

8. Eckhart Tolle, *A New Earth: Awakening to Your Life's Purpose* (New York: Penguin, 2006), 219.

9. Ibid., 71.

10. Quoted in Carrington Steele, *Don't Drink the Kool-Aid: Oprah, Obama and the Occult* (Scotts Valley, CA: CreateSpace, 2008), 41.

11. Tolle, 267.

12. Marianne Williamson, *A Return to Love* (New York: HarperCollins, 1996), 19.

13. Ibid., 31.

14. Ibid., 33.

15. Schucman, Workbook for Students, 58.

16. Rhonda Byrne, *The Secret* (New York: Atria Books, 2006), 28.

17. Ibid.,164.

18. Ibid.,183.

19. John Ankerberg and John Weldon, *Encyclopedia of Cults and New Religions* (Eugene, OR: Harvest House, 1999), 297.

20. Tolle, 196.

21. Schucman, Workbook for Students, 471.

22. Tolle , 13.

23. Ibid., 68, 69.

Chapter 3: Redefining Conversion

1. Eckhart Tolle, *A New Earth: Awakening to Your Life's Purpose* (New York: Penguin, 2006), 23.

2. Quoted in Carrington Steele, *Don't Drink the Kool-Aid: Oprah, Obama and the Occult* (Scotts Valley, CA: CreateSpace, 2008), 41.

3. Tolle, 260.

4. Helen Schucman, *A Course in Miracles: Text, Workbook for Students, Manual for Teachers* (Glen Ellen, CA: The Foundation for Inner Peace, 1977), Manual for Teachers, 58.

5. Ibid., Text, 37.

6. Ibid., 57.

7. Marianne Williamson, *A Return to Love* (New York: HarperCollins, 1996), 298, 299.

8. Steele, 24.

9. C. S. Lewis, *The Screwtape Letters* (New York: Macmillan, 1943), 39.

10. Tolle, 225.

11. Tolle, 259.

12. Schucman, Manual for Teachers, 364.

13. Tolle, 76.

14. "One Way or Many Ways? The Gospel According to Oprah," Watchman Fellowship, transcribed from video clip, http://www.watchman.org/oprah.htm.

Chapter 4: Redefining Death

1. Helen Schucman, *A Course in Miracles: Text, Workbook for Students, Manual for Teachers* (Glen Ellen, CA: The Foundation for Inner Peace, 1977), Manual for Teachers, 66.

2. Ibid., 61.

3. Ibid., 66.

4. Schucman, Workbook for Students, 309.

5. Schucman, Manual for Teachers, 67.

6. Marianne Williamson, *A Return to Love* (New York: HarperCollins, 1996), 126.

7. Eckhart Tolle, *A New Earth: Awakening to Your Life's Purpose* (New York: Penguin, 2006), 23.

8. Schucman, Text, 187.

9. Williamson, 243.

10. Ibid., 244–245.

11. Schucman, Text, 34.

12. Williamson, 20.

Chapter 5: Redefining Morality

1. Eckhart Tolle, *A New Earth: Awakening to Your Life's Purpose* (New York: Penguin, 2006), 163.

2. Ibid., 196.

3. Ibid., 13.

4. Marianne Williamson, *A Return to Love* (New York: HarperCollins, 1996), 97.

5. See Tolle, 73, 76.

6. Dave Hunt and T. A. McMahon, *America, The Sorcerer's New Apprentice: The Rise of New Age Shamanism* (Eugene, OR: Harvest House, 1988), 223.

7. Williamson, 19–20.

8. Rhonda Byrne, *The Secret* (New York: Atria Books, 2006), 26.

9. SPC Newsletter, 1982, 2.

10. Byrne, 40.

11. Ibid., 45.

12. Ibid., 48.

13. Ibid., 58.

14. Helen Schucman, *A Course in Miracles: Text, Workbook for Students, Manual for Teachers* (Glen Ellen, CA: The Foundation for Inner Peace, 1977), Text, 264.

15. Quoted in Carrington Steele, *Don't Drink the Kool-Aid: Oprah, Obama and the Occult* (Scotts Valley, CA: CreateSpace, 2008), 29.

Chapter 6: The Lie and the End Times

1. For the complete story of this spear read Trevor Ravenscroft, *The Spear of Destiny* (York Beach, Maine: Samuel Weiser, 1982).

2. Ravenscroft, 65.

3. Ibid., 92.

4. Gerald Suster, *Hitler: The Occult Messiah* (New York: St. Martin's, 1981), 120.

5. Helen Schucman, *A Course in Miracles: Text, Workbook for Students, Manual for Teachers* (Glen Ellen, CA: The Foundation for Inner Peace, 1977), Manual for Teachers, 58.

6. Quoted in Carrington Steele, *Don't Drink the Kool-Aid: Oprah, Obama and the Occult* (Scotts Valley, CA: CreateSpace, 2008), 31.

7. Eckhart Tolle, *A New Earth* (New York: Penguin, 2006), 71.

8. Schucman, Workbook for Students, 364.

IS GOD ON AMERICA'S SIDE?

ISBN-13: 978-0-8024-8952-4

With characteristic wisdom and lucidity, Dr. Erwin W. Lutzer addresses a fundamental question—a question begging for an answer after a frenetic election—is God really on America's side? Lutzer provides insights on how Christians should view government and teaches how "to think with the Bible in one hand and a newspaper in the other."

MOODY
PUBLISHERS.

1-800-678-8812 · MOODYPUBLISHERS.COM

THE TRUTH ABOUT
SAME-SEX MARRIAGE

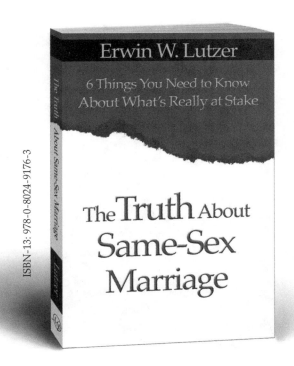

ISBN-13: 978-0-8024-9176-3

Dr. Erwin W. Lutzer, pastor of the Moody Church in Chicago and esteemed theologian, responds to the attacks that marriage has sustained over the past several years. His answers will help you formulate your own answers to outspoken opponents of the biblical definition of marriage.

 MOODY
PUBLISHERS.

1-800-678-8812 · MOODYPUBLISHERS.COM

SEVEN REASONS WHY YOU CAN TRUST THE BIBLE

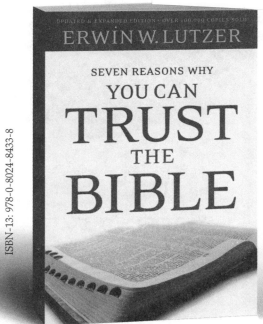

With the cultural onslaught against the authority of God's Word, explore the seven reasons why we can unequivocally trust and fully depend on the Bible. *Seven Reasons Why You Can Trust the Bible* is revised, expanded, and includes Bible study questions at the end of each chapter. It is an effective resource for the lay Christian who desires to understand why we believe what we believe.

MOODY
PUBLISHERS.

1-800-678-8812 · MOODYPUBLISHERS.COM